Copyright © 1971 by Bernarda Sharkey, O.S.B.
Photographs copyright © 1971 by Marion Faller.
All rights reserved.

All photographs herein are the property of Marion Faller except those on pages 7, 10, 21, 26, 42, 43, 48, 76, which were supplied by the author.

Library of Congress
Catalog Card Number: 77-156493

Published by Paulist Press
Editorial Office: 304 W. 58th St., N.Y., N.Y. 10019
Business Office: 400 Sette Dr., Paramus, N.J. 07652

Printed and bound in the
United States of America

An Education to Wonder Book

GROWING TO WONDER

Handbook for Parents

By Bernarda Sharkey
Photographs by Marion Faller
Designed by Judith Savard, R.S.H.M.
Education to Wonder Series Director:
   Richard J. Payne

PAULIST PRESS
New York/Paramus, N.J./Toronto

Author's Acknowledgments

Across the years there have been many persons who have been and are sources of delight and wonder but time and space limit the inclusion of all their names here. There are, however, those who must be named:

My parents, the A. J. Sharkeys; my sister and her family, the David Phipps family.

The families who let me play with their children so I could put into words the experience of a child's wonder: the Gary Dark family, the Riley Fell family, the Ed Grewe family, the Bill Myers family and the Henry Scroggins family.

My community, the Sisters of Benedict, and in particular Sisters Miriam Schnoebelen, Marie Ballmann, Mary Charles Bryce, Joan Dark, Denise Mohr, Lucy Krieser, and Mary Frances Swanda.

Co-workers in the Office of Religious Education: Rev. Bernard Jewitt, Carole Molyneaux, Mrs. Nora Lafferty, and Sisters Marcelline Niemann and Marita Ganley.

And other friends, especially Barb Schumacher, Carolyn Sugg Sherman, the Phil Pedicords, Fathers Paul Maier, James Halpine, David Jones, Tom Stafford, Lowell Stieferman, John Costanzo, and Daniel Brown.

Contents

Why Wonder? 8

Awareness/Absorption 22

Play as Learning 32

Children and Art 42

Projects in Delight 54

What We Want for Our Children 70

Your Own Chapter 84

Once when I was six years old I saw a magnificent picture in a book, called *True Stories from Nature,* about the primeval forest. It was a picture of a boa constrictor in the act of swallowing an animal. . . .

In the book it said: "Boa constrictors swallow their prey whole, without chewing it. After that they are not able to move, and they sleep through the six months that they need for digestion."

I pondered deeply, then, over the adventures of the jungle. And after some work with a colored pencil I succeeded in making my first drawing. . . .

I showed my masterpiece to the grown-ups, and asked them whether the drawing frightened them.

But they answered: "Frighten? Why should anyone be frightened by a hat?"

My drawing was not a picture of a hat. It was a picture of a boa constrictor digesting an elephant. But since the grown-ups were not able to understand it, I made another drawing: I drew the inside of the boa constrictor, so that the grown-ups could see it clearly. They always need to have things explained. . . .

The grown-ups' response, this time, was to advise me to lay aside my drawings of boa constrictors, whether from the inside or the outside, and devote myself instead to geography, history, arithmetic, and grammar. That is why, at the age of six, I gave up what might have been a magnificent career as a painter. I had been disheartened by the failure of my Drawing Number One and my Drawing Number Two. Grown-ups never understand anything by themselves, and it is tiresome for children to be always and forever explaining things to them. . . .

Grown-ups love figures. When you tell them that you have made a new friend, they never ask you any questions about essential matters. They never say to you, "What does his voice sound like? What games does he love best? Does he collect butterflies?" Instead, they demand: "How old is he? How many brothers has he? How much does he weigh? How much money does his father make?" Only from these figures do they think they have learned anything about him.

If you were to say to the grown-ups: "I saw a beautiful house made of rosy brick, with geraniums in the windows and doves on the roof," they would not be able to get any idea of that house at all. You would have to say to them: "I saw a house that cost $20,000." Then they would exclaim: "Oh, what a pretty house that is!"...

They are like that. One must not hold it against them. Children should always show great forbearance toward grown-up people.

From The Little Prince by Antoine de Saint-Exupéry, translated by Katherine Woods, copyright, 1943, by Harcourt, Brace & World, Inc. and reprinted with their permission.

Why Wonder?

To see the world in beauty, in delight: this is what the young years are for, what the wonder years are about—to shape children's sense of wonder, of delight, of beauty.

Wonder Bread ads say it perfectly. Rachel Carson hoped for it in her lovely book *The Sense of Wonder:*

> "A child's world is fresh and new and beautiful, full of wonder and excitement. It is our misfortune that for most of us that clear-eyed vision, that true instinct for what is beautiful and awe-inspiring, is dimmed and even lost before we reach adulthood. If I had influence with the good fairy who is to preside over the christening of all children, I should ask that her gift to each child in the world would be a sense of wonder so indestructible that it would last throughout life, as an unfailing antidote against boredom and disenchantment of later years."

Other writers who point to the need for the development of wonder are Ignace Lepp, Erich Fromm, John Gardner, Robert Johann, and Clark Moustakas, to name but a few.

Ignace Lepp in *The Philosophy of Existence* states this simply: "From the first moment when man appreciates beauty, he makes the first breach in the imprisoning wall of the everyday."

Statistics show that a five-year-old child is 90 percent creative; at age seven the percentage drops to 10 percent, and by the age of eight or nine the creative potential of the child has been seriously undermined. Most adults operate at a 2 percent creative level. Why?

Educators say many factors are detrimental to the child's growth in wonder and in his ability to express his own powers of creativity. One of the most evident is the pressure to conform, which may come from many directions. Ridicule, an over-emphasis on rewards or success, authoritarian attitudes and environments are also damaging to a child's growth in wonder and delight.

But why should we be concerned about fostering wonder and creativity? Is it vital for maturity, for fullness of manhood or womanhood? Is education for wonder a part of education for assuming responsibility as a citizen, as a parent, as an adult in society?

Psychologists say wonder is one of the key ingredients in the formation of a whole person. Abraham Maslow, the renowned psychologist, says: "Creativeness must ultimately be defined as the coming to pass of the fullest humanness." And any sense of creation—from an appreciation of its beauty to expressing it in oneself—has to do with wonder.

Clark Moustakas further describes the mature human as "a real individual who approaches life with an openness of self, a touching, groping, feeling, sensing, reaching, and tasting orientation. He perceives all significant experiences fully and completely with sensitivity to a great variety of internal and external cues."

Erich Fromm believes that the creative force in man is the root of either creativity or destructiveness, that destructiveness occurs when the creative potential has not been fostered or developed or when it has been hampered.

John Gardner, writing in *Time* magazine, April, 1969, says: "The society capable of continuous renewal will be one that develops to the fullest its human resources, that removes obstacles to individual fulfillment, that emphasizes education, life-long learning and self-discovery."

The years of growing up are precisely those years in which the power and sense of wonder is one of the most important tools available to parents and teachers for fulfillment of the kind of growth Gardner writes about. Parents and teachers can give children the kind of encouragement vital to their becoming full persons simply by providing a warm, accepting atmosphere. Nurture of the sense of wonder means using the tools of discovery, awareness, delight, reverence, surprise, which are part and parcel of children's experiences on a daily basis. All that has to happen is that this be fostered, be accepted, be encouraged.

The environment for wonder and creativity is an atmosphere of warmth, of love and acceptance, an atmosphere of freedom. Harold Anderson terms it "the open system" which he calls "like sunlight in which growing things grow." What we are trying to do with children at this age is to make them aware, keenly aware, of everything that is. Play, fun, work, life, family, pets—all things that make up the ritual of everyday life are the only tools that are needed to make reverence, silence, awe, delight possible.

Educators define five levels of creativity: expressive, productive, inventive, innovative, and emergentive. Emergentive is the final level, one which we may define as Christian maturity, for it is the highest form of creativity. It is the ability to absorb ordinary experiences and from these to change the ordinary situation. This level forms the basis for a man's ability to change society, to change structures, to have the courage to remain committed to the ideals in which he believes, whatever the cost may be.

We begin training children for this goal by working with them on the expressive level—a level which is natural for them during their years of growth and development. Expressive creativity opens persons to new possibilities for growth in their own creative patterns; this in turn prepares them for the next level of growth. Responsible commitment and continual growing in life's process are the fruit of such formation. We may say, then, that preparing children for wonder and creativity is a formation for Christian maturity.

GROWTH IN WONDER

A teleiodoscope is a type of kaleidoscope that breaks up and rearranges the patterns of objects around you. It is a good example of what growth in wonder is all about. Find one or buy one (they're not expensive) and look around you. Look at the window, the floor, the chairs, trees, sunlight, dishes, animals. Most of all, look at people. To look at something in the light of the teleiodoscope is to see it for the first time, to see it in exciting dimensions, to see it as beautiful even when you know it may be just a piece of paper or your shoes. And life looks so much better after you have seen something old in a new way. You see things in a new light.

Children using the teleiodoscope find everything more exciting than usual. Four-year-old Gerard looked at the plant in the living room, saying, "It's so pretty," and Mary, a third-grader, could only exclaim "Oh, neat! Oh, neat!"

For your children, your being *there* in their lives is the most important factor in developing their sense of wonder. That may seem overstated, but it is mostly a matter of sharing—sharing in the sense of your taking time with them. You don't have to provide toys or instructions on how to play; you might just sit quietly while they play with the dog, or walk through the park with them to see the leaves in autumn.

For example, recently Gerard brought in several pieces of string. His mother did not tell him or his sisters Monica and Grace how to play with them.

She sat and watched them sort out colors. Grace decided she wanted to learn to braid; Gerard began trying to tie a knot for his truck-line; Mary began making a picture on the floor with several pieces. After some moments when all three children were totally absorbed in what they were doing, Mary and Gerard made a jump rope out of the yarn and went outside to use it. Gerard tied one end to a rail and began turning it for Monica. All of this happened without any word from their mother—only her presence and interest in what they were doing. When they began jumping rope, she went out and suggested that they might move to another place where they wouldn't fall on the cement.

Children are impulsive, impatient, and your working with them in this area demands a lot of patience on your part. For one thing, they usually don't want to play with whatever toys you may bring out for them or suggest. They often will play with a piece of cardboard or a discarded kitchen utensil.

Clark Moustakas describes the kind of attitude necessary for forming a sense of wonder: it is an inclination to take life as an adventure and a becoming; it is having a sense of curiosity and a willingness to understand what's going on in oneself and in related aspects of the environment, having an interest in new ideas and fresh perspectives, a spirit of play and experimentation.

Perhaps the most important thing you can do is listen to your children. Listen to their discoveries: "Mom, look at the caterpillar on the step. Mom, I found out today how to spell my name. Dad, why does it help the car to have oil put in it?" To listen to your children demands that you really sit down and get to know them as people—as precious persons of infinite potential.

In our day and age we hear a lot of discussion of the "generation gap." If you don't listen to your children during the "wonder years," the generation gap will yawn wider than ever. Communication between parents and their children becomes more difficult during the adolescent years; listening to them when they want to share beauty and discovery and delight is part of preparation for being there during all the important moments of their years, both now and in the future.

With the research and studies being done on education, on creativity, and on teaching, scholars are discovering that the key to it all is the *attitude* of the teacher or parent. An openness to the other —in this case, the child—is the basis for his becoming a person who can believe in himself, who can begin to use his God-given abilities. The most influential factor in his becoming a well-integrated mature person is your belief in him as a person of worth and value, your encouraging his discovery of the wonderful world around him. If you criticize him for his failures, pressure him to be like his brothers or his cousins, or refuse to try to understand his side, you will lessen him in his own eyes and make him feel unworthy. Part of his growth in wonder comes from your discovering beauty with him.

Wonder is everywhere you look. It is a further way. It is discovering something new each day. It means seeing all the loveliness in things like mud puddles, rainy days, darkness. This is what poetry is about: E. E. Cummings, Teilhard de Chardin, Antoine de Saint Exupéry, Mr. Blue, Corita Kent, The Red Balloon, Martin Buber, Gerard Manley Hopkins. You have an infinite array of choices for finding what appeals to you.

Sometimes people are afraid that in teaching children about joy, we may be failing to tell them that life is hard, that there is pain in the world. The sense of wonder, of discovery, of delight is probably the most valuable lesson that we can give children in learning to cope with the pain of life. Becoming refreshed, learning to celebrate life fully is a source of strength for us. It is the measure of resurrection that makes a Calvary endurable.

One of the most important ingredients for cultivating wonder in the child is freedom. This means freedom—psychologically, physically, and realistically. Frequently adults believe that freedom for children means a total lack of discipline or too much permissiveness. What freedom, in the best sense, boils down to is letting a child become himself. It means not putting our own labels on what he is doing—"No, Jimmy, skies are *blue*. Ugh, what an ugly worm, Billy; get rid of it. Sally, nice little girls don't play with footballs." Haim Ginnott has some principles and advice that are of real value for parents and teachers. Perhaps what adults need to remember about children is that they are persons and deserve to be treated accordingly.

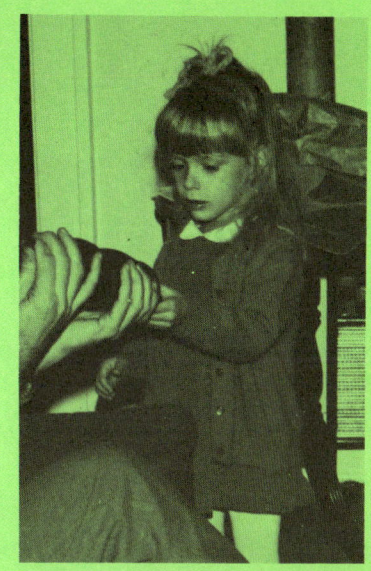

Awareness/Absorption

Our environment is anything about us; that's rather obvious. We are always learning from it. Always. Perhaps that's obvious but it is startling too. We learn all the time without ever being aware of it.

And the child is absorbing everything about him: home, smells, sunlight, sounds, trees, persons, dogs, attitudes, feelings. He has invisible antennae that pick up, literally, everything—and frequently the things that are most hidden to us.

The old story about little pitchers having big ears well describes the fact that children absorb anything and everything about them. As parents and educators, we are concerned that what they absorb is healthy and meaningful, full of possibilities for developing them as Christian persons. It is not possible or desirable for them to grow up in airtight compartments where they are free from all elements which seem undesirable. What we have to do is to help them become aware of the good things, to see all the beauty and wonder there is, along with what is not so beautiful and wonderful, and to help them learn to make choices and decisions based on value

judgments. This seems to be a simple formula, but any parent or teacher knows it is a tremendous task.

Marshall McLuhan describes the artist as "the man of integral awareness." Many educators describe every person as potential artist. If we believe a child is an artist in germ, someone whom we lead toward adulthood by fostering awareness, we begin to understand that what Abraham Heschel describes as the goal of religious education—"a sensitivity to wonder and the capacity for radical amazement"—means this everyday world where we and our children live.

A child is always learning. Period. Think about that. He is learning when he gets up in the morning, when he puts on his shoes, brushes his teeth, eats breakfast, and ventures forth on his business of the day. Each activity in his life, each person he meets, each moment and whatever it holds, is telling him things. He is discovering what he himself, what his life, what the world are all about. He is learning this information from the atmosphere he is in, from the sounds of voices, from the warmth and love evidenced by concrete terms. How you feel about him comes through in rather ordinary symbols: cereal for breakfast, clean clothes, the hug you give him when he comes into the kitchen, the way you look at him when he tells you about the squirrel he saw in the tree. He is learning about the world from his walk to school, the pieces of information he catches from television or radio, from the way other persons—the milkman, the policeman, the neighbors, his teacher, his friends—act and react to situ-

ations. He is learning how all of life works: how flowers grow, how kites fly, how dogs run, how boys play ball, how families are for loving.

A child may wander to school and be late because he stopped to watch a frog on the sidewalk or the way the lights change at the corner. Did you ever notice how the cars bolt forward like a herd of mechanical monsters controlled by the green and red lights? Ask your son or daughter what it looks like. A little girl may be so involved in the game of house she is playing that she literally does not hear the dinner call or her mother's voice telling her to put away her toys. Being absorbed is part of being young.

A child's sense of awareness, of being able to become totally absorbed in what he is doing, can be a valuable tool. Intensifying it by sharing it with him or by calling his attention to something beautiful or startling gives these moments more importance, more clarification. Rachel Carson, in *The Sense of Wonder*, says: "Exploring nature with your child is largely a matter of becoming receptive to what lies all around you. You can drink in beauty and think and wonder at the meaning of what you see."

Such an experience requires shutting out other noises, other sights, and just seeing, perhaps for the first time, what cement looks like, how rain smells, what bark looks like. It means rediscovering the world.

The ability to concentrate is really built into the very fiber of a person. The problem is that we sometimes want children to concentrate on things which seem unworthy of their time and effort; it would be much more sensible and meaningful for them to concentrate on things which compel their attention. A lot of educational research today points to this very fact: that by forcing children to become bored and unchallenged through the enforced learning of unworthwhile things, we have destroyed their capacity to wonder, their ability to become involved and absorbed in really exciting learning.

One author, George Leonard, describes true education as ecstasy. Much of the ecstasy, the delight in learning, has been on the sly, has been despite school, has been a bootleg product. It is a bit startling but true that wherever there is delight, there is learning. Corita Kent describes the kind of experience anyone can gain from such a trek into beauty: "To really see what we ordinarily look at from time to time makes fireworks happen inside us that can't always be contained when the brightness of a person or thing is discovered or uncovered."

This becomes even more important to the child when it is shared with others. Parents are the first in line to be so favored with such delight. George Leonard says: "Parents have the very first opportunity to create joyful and effective learning environments for their children. From the beginning they can reinforce exploratory behavior in every child. Parents who are truly in touch with their children can set up the kinds of environments that will bring forth remarkable, constructive, and involving behaviors."

Guy Yves Jacquin in *The Psychology of the School-Age Child* makes some observations along these same lines:

> "Only in a common spirit of discovery, with an insatiable curiosity stemming from respect and admiration for a creation ceaselessly renewed, will we lead the child to the discovery of the world in which he lives. And in this way we ourselves will go on to the discovery of the heart of the child, and go on with him to the discovery of an ideal which will enthrall our youth and lead us toward an identical star. For it is really our youthfulness of heart which will give him this mentality of an explorer and a discoverer of miracles."

Appreciation of art or poetry or any form of beauty is really the means of keeping alive man's inborn sense of beauty. Children are natural artists, natural poets, natural beauty-lovers, and will continue to express all of these qualities in themselves and in their lives if we give them the kind of help they need to keep these gifts alive. The way to keep something alive is to cherish it, to care for it, to guard it, to watch it with gentleness and let it grow. This is precisely how we keep alive our children's poetry, art, the beauty inherent in their very beings. We presume it is there, wrapped carefully inside them, like a gift we must not break or handle roughly, but only unwrap softly, gently—the way a rose opens when spring comes.

Play as Learning

Play and childhood seem almost synonymous, yet too few of us realize how intrinsic to the learning process is the whole business of play. Much research on the value of play for adults as well as children is being done today. Theologians such as Hugo Rahner see it as a core of man's make-up and point to play as the quality wherein man is like God.

Schiller says man is perfectly human only when he plays.

For a child, play is his everyday world. Sam Keen says: "The child tends to think in terms of the logic of play about the whole world." Play gives a child a sense of awareness of his body when he climbs, jumps, runs, or uses his physical powers in any way. In play a child arranges objects so that he is the boss, so he can master his own life situation.

A child's play begins with and centers on his own body. As an infant, he explores the world through his perception of himself. Later on he plays with available persons and things. His small world of toys is something like a harbor where he finds sanctuary and safety. Playfulness is the mode of his relationship with others.

As he grows he discovers which things are real and which are fantasy. The child learns to deal with reality through his play. It is the norm of life for him and the means by which he is able to cope with situations. By experiment and planning, he is able to master this world. In such a way he is able to achieve a success and enter the next phase of his development. Play is vital to his growth as a person who is able to succeed at each step upward to adulthood.

Physical touching is a child's testing mechanism in operation. He feels, gropes, stretches, sees life only through his own body. As he experiences, he is absorbing much that he may not be able to verbalize as yet. But the sensitizing that is happening at this time has an impact on the whole of his life.

J. Nina Liberman defines playfulness as "1, spontaneity and ease and freedom of movement; 2, joy expressed through delight, liking, smiling, laughter; 3, a sense of humor which is often expressed through teasing." Erik Erikson claims that a child uses play to gain control over his environment, while Jean Piaget suggests that the playing child is testing the environment in order to know how to deal with it.

A child's curiosity and wonder lead him to explore his world and to delight in everything he finds. He is intensely absorbed in whatever is.

By shaping materials and things, man is shaping himself as well. When a child learns to use and touch things in a reverent, loving way he begins to see how to use the world and time and all materials in a loving way. Education is taking place all the time, not just when we set up a situation where we believe the child is learning. He learns always and everywhere. The only requirements are his involvement, how important to him the situation is, and that he be thinking about what he is doing. Discovery is the primary mode of education, whether it is simply finding something anew or whether it is asking questions. For the child, discovery happens every day. It is a matter of finding newness at every turn. Parents and teachers only have to be there as guides and sharers of this adventure in learning.

Knowing how to play with a child is knowing how to gain his confidence. He learns almost totally by experiencing with his senses. His curiosity enables him to discover the whole world. Adults need only to be willing to spend time and themselves in order to rediscover a world they had forgotten, and the preciousness of a person in the child.
Jacquin says:

> "Games put all the child's faculties to work. They provide exercise for his body and training for his muscles which attain strength and suppleness, his physique which acquires solidity and his nervous reflexes which become rapid, precise, and effective only to the extent that he uses them frequently at play. A child really understands only what he does, only what he lives. Playing is all of this. It is the right fuel for his spirit.

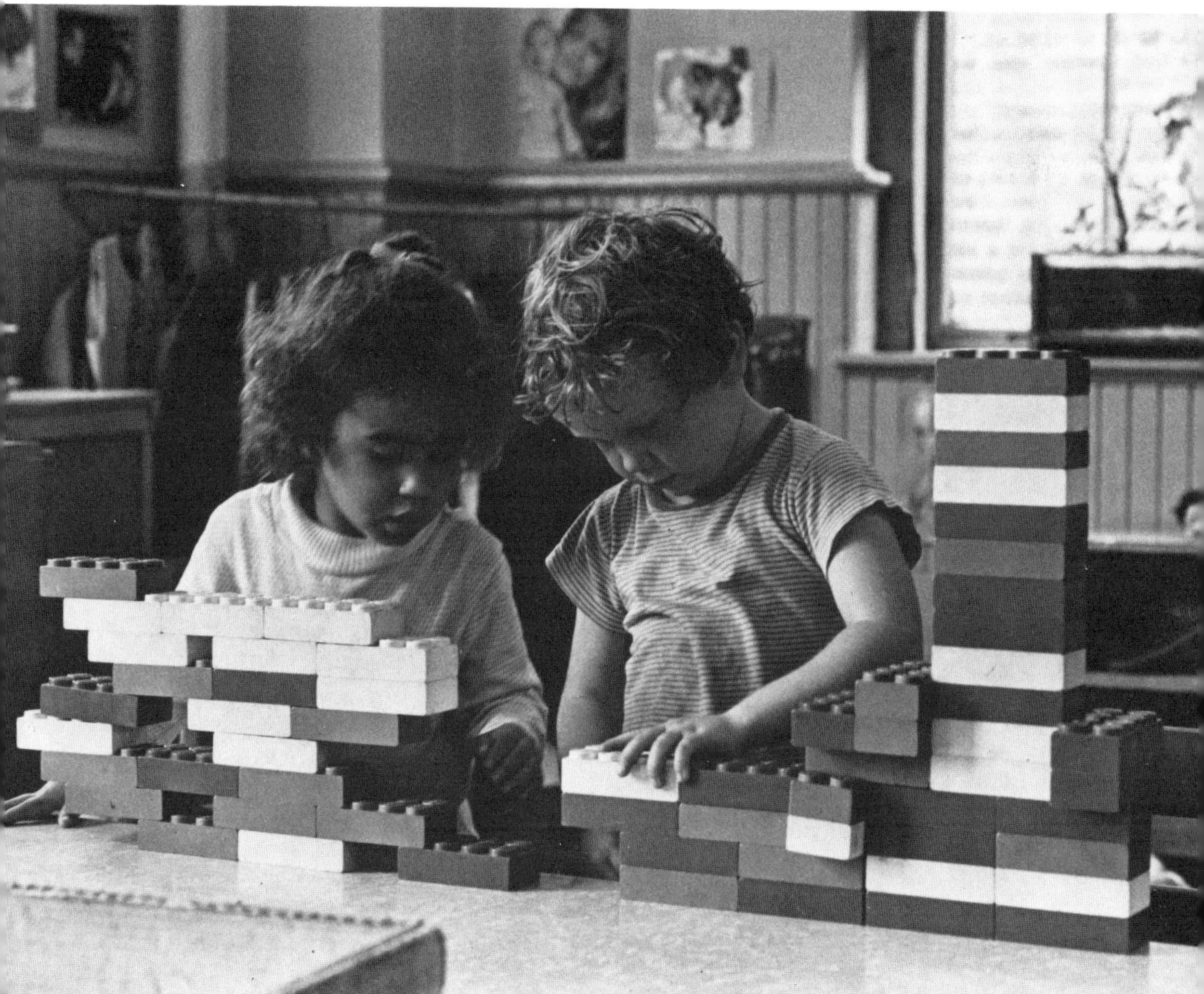

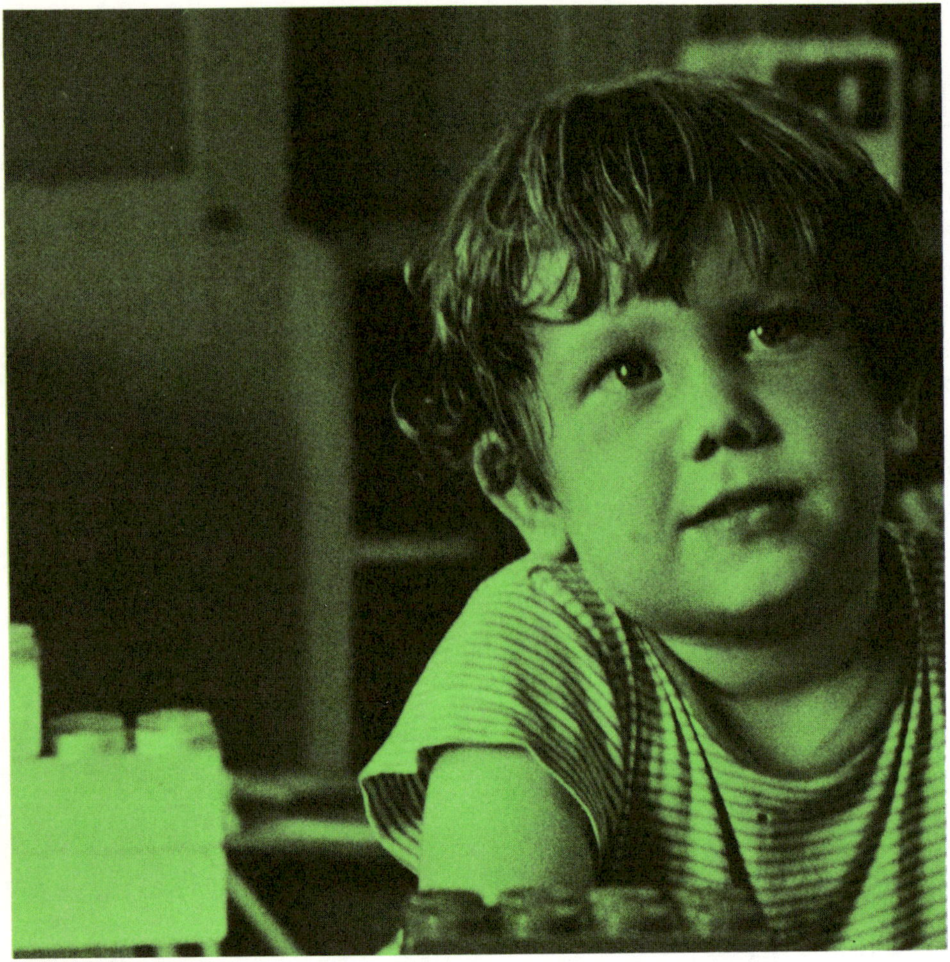

"If the child's mind is working and if his fingers, eyes, or ears are busy, you must realize that nothing is useless for him that can give him a new idea or a new experience. Let him be—whether he is dissecting a tree leaf with his awkward fingers, or using a pebble on a hard rock, or following the chimney smoke with his eyes. This is the way he will learn things that we know, or that we do not know and will never know. He is building the universe. And our role is never to arrest his effort and perseverance but to encourage and channel it always."

Too often we associate wonder only with childhood, and even then we become impatient when our children find life so full of wonder. In a book entitled *Apology for Wonder*, theologian Sam Keen makes the point that wonder is part and parcel of faith, that it is in seeing life as a gift, in seeing the world as wonderful, that man is able to believe in a creator. If this is so, a child's experience of wonder is a basic tool for his formation as a believer.

A wondering attitude means that one delights in life, finds life meaningful, life hopeful, life worth living. This kind of attitude is rarely found today, even among Christians. Despair, anxiety, hopelessness are common in our world, although we have progressed technologically beyond any other period in history, although man has reached a peak never known before. In wonder we touch the world with awe, with delight, with an attitude that lets it—nature, person, other—be itself. Wonder is man's reaction to what is sacred and holy; it evokes a meaningfulness in our attitudes and prevents our seeing the other as an object or as something merely useful to us. Wonder implies a base of seeing life as gift, of seeing others as giftedness, of viewing whatever happens with surprise—with a kind of humor and playfulness that is bound up with a very healthy attitude toward life.

A child's natural attitude is wonder. Everything looks new to him—even if he sees it every day—and he never ceases marvelling at how beautiful things are. Everyone and everything is good.

"This sense of delight in the child," says Sam Keen, "is bound up with the possibility of action, mastery, and control. The mastery of novelty is one of the most constant sources of childhood delight and wonder. One might almost measure the psychic health of a child by the number of times his eyes sparkle with the triumphant affirmation: 'I did it! I did it!'"

One way parents force children to lose their sense of wonder is by fostering a sense of failure, so that a child feels unable to deal with his world. There are many ways parents can do this; the primary way is through rejection of a child, the refusal to love a child for himself. A parent who truly loves his child will see him as he is and give him the sense of security and worthwhileness that is absolutely necessary for him to mature with serenity and to be able to achieve in life.

Another way parents wrong their children is by refusing to let them play. They may believe that play is unworthy of the time spent on it or improper for children of a particular age. Play is part and parcel of childhood and should be valued for its own sake. It is the medium of learning for the child, and as such it needs no other excuse for being. Play is a child's workaday world. It is the means for his spontaneous acceptance of reality and for his learning to fulfill himself and his world.

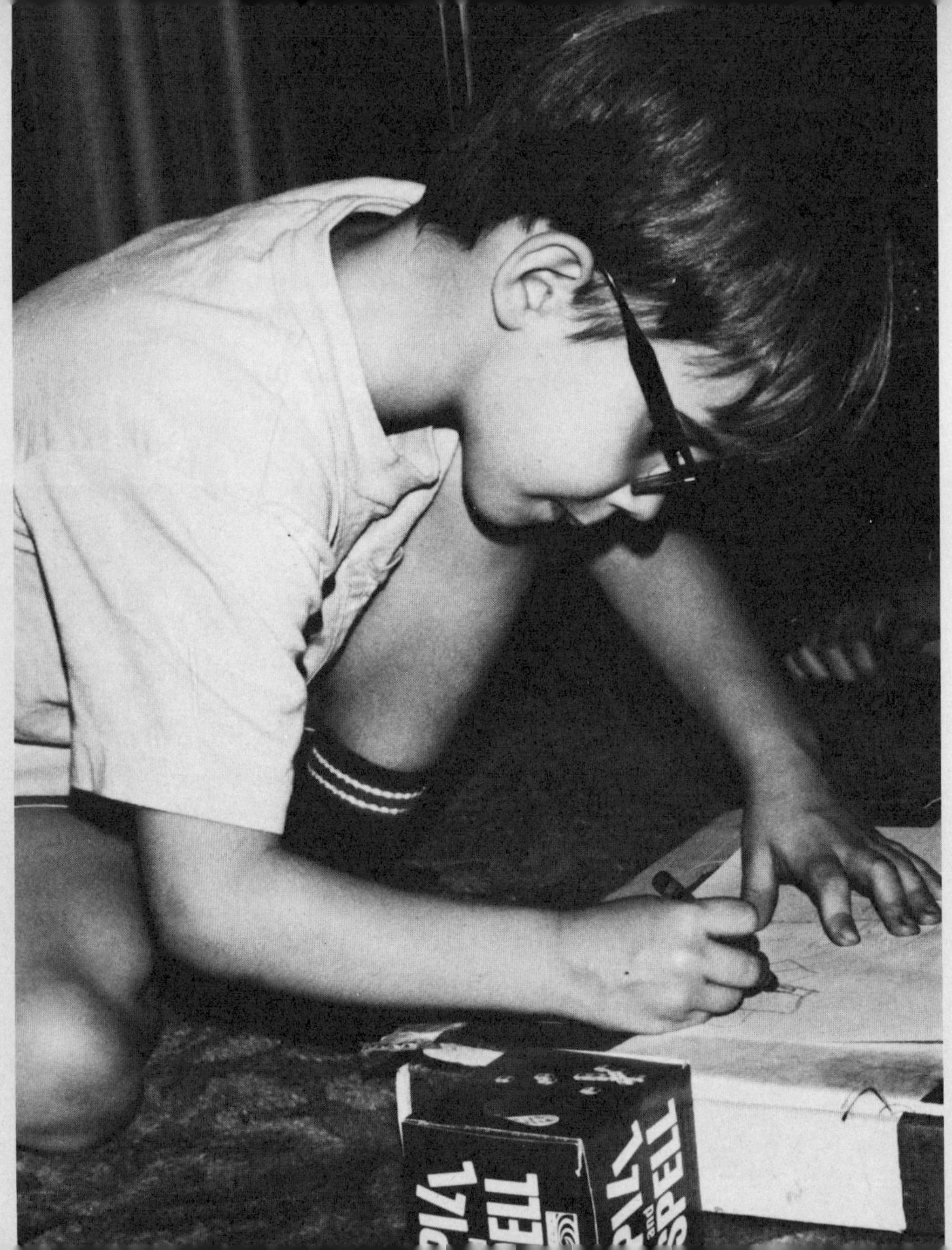

Children and Art

Drawing is one of the most important media of expression. Drawing is a true, direct, immediate expression of what the child is perceiving. Any form of artistic expression gives evidence of deep personal feelings and intuitions. For a child, art work is the most direct "verbalization" of what he knows and how he sees.

Some religious educators even see art work for a child as a directly religious experience. Certainly it has possibilities of being this, just as any true human experience can be religious if it is seen in its Christian context—if it is seen as expressing what is deeply beautiful and human and believing.

A child draws, colors, and paints what he sees, just as the adult says what he sees, or a dancer dances, a poet sings, a musician takes to the keyboard or strings. In such a way, a child does what is most natural for him as his means of saying it. He draws.

Drawing is a way of achieving success, of expressing emotions, of shaping ideas and of acquiring some skill. Every child is a potential artist if he is not discouraged by being told he is unable to draw like his brother, or that he can't draw a straight line.

What is important is that he be given the opportunity to express his feelings. Art is highly desirable for children of any age and is an activity they take to naturally.

Victor Lowenfield, the art educator, believes that education in art provides a catalyst for all education, that by artistic expression a person is able to integrate all of his experiences and is somehow brought to his finest development as a person. Drawing is a medium of expression of what life means to a child. Much work has been done in psychology on the use of color, and the way trees, people, sky are drawn. All these reflect the expression of the emotional and psychological development of the person. Beyond this, however, drawing is an important part of childhood for any person, something parents can share with their children in a very simple way. Parents can provide tools such as crayons or paint and the time to sit down with them.

A child does express many things through drawing which he could never say in words, things that go far beyond words. For drawing is both words and gestures. It expresses actions, people, ideas, reality, all at once. It expresses a dimension of the person that cannot be told any other way. Drawing says person in a way nothing else can say it. Sometimes we adults are too busy or too dense to read the message that is waiting to be read by us.

Drawings are expressions of a child's personality. It is not very important whether they reflect great artistic ability in terms of skill or promise,

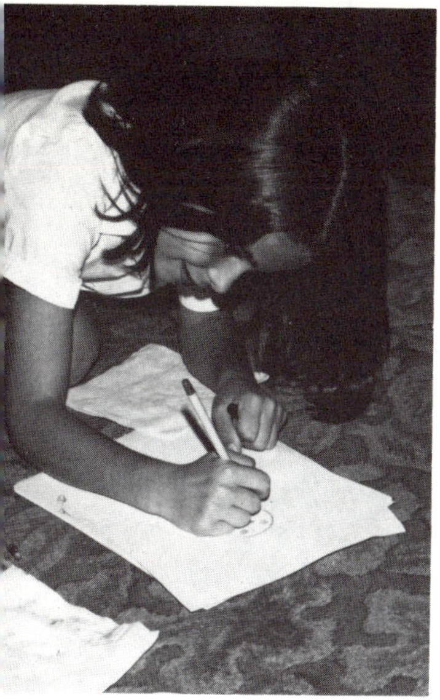
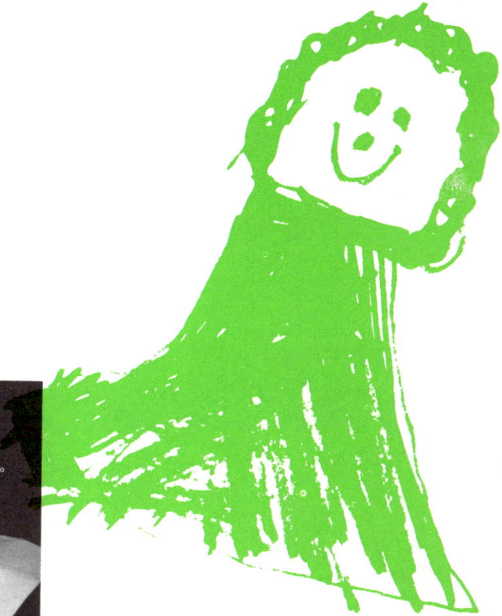
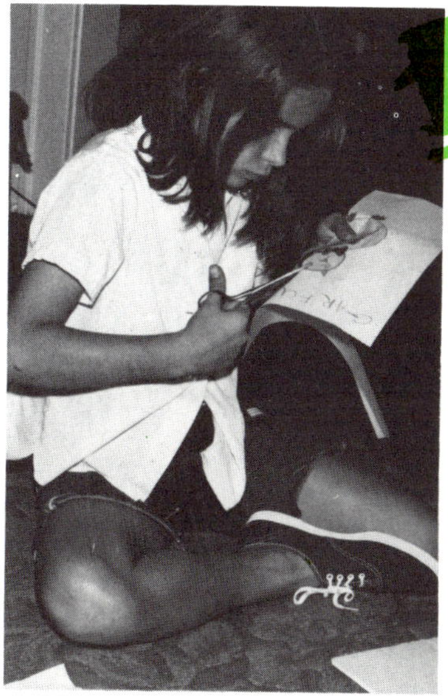
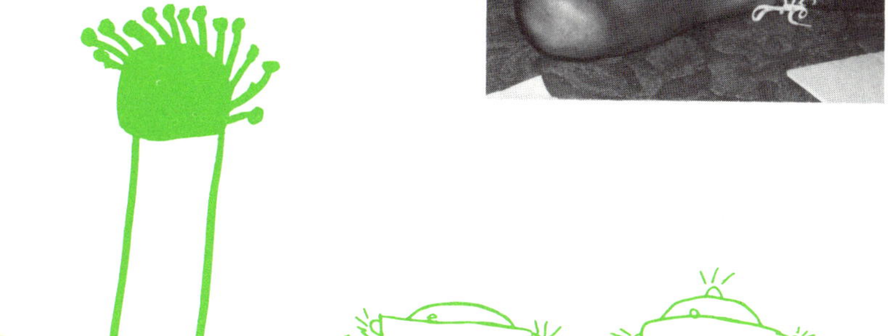
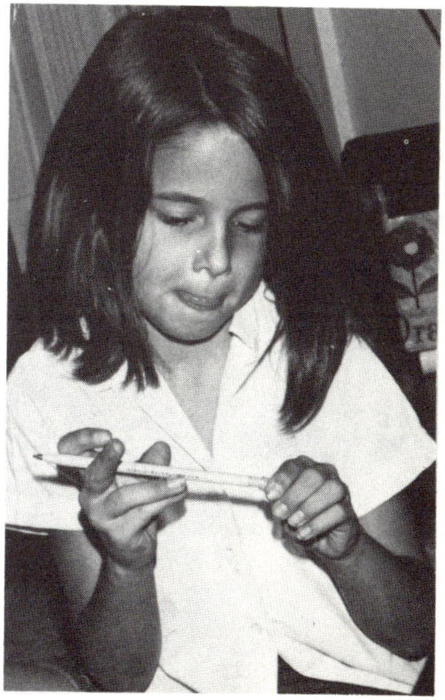

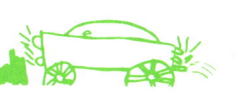

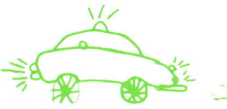

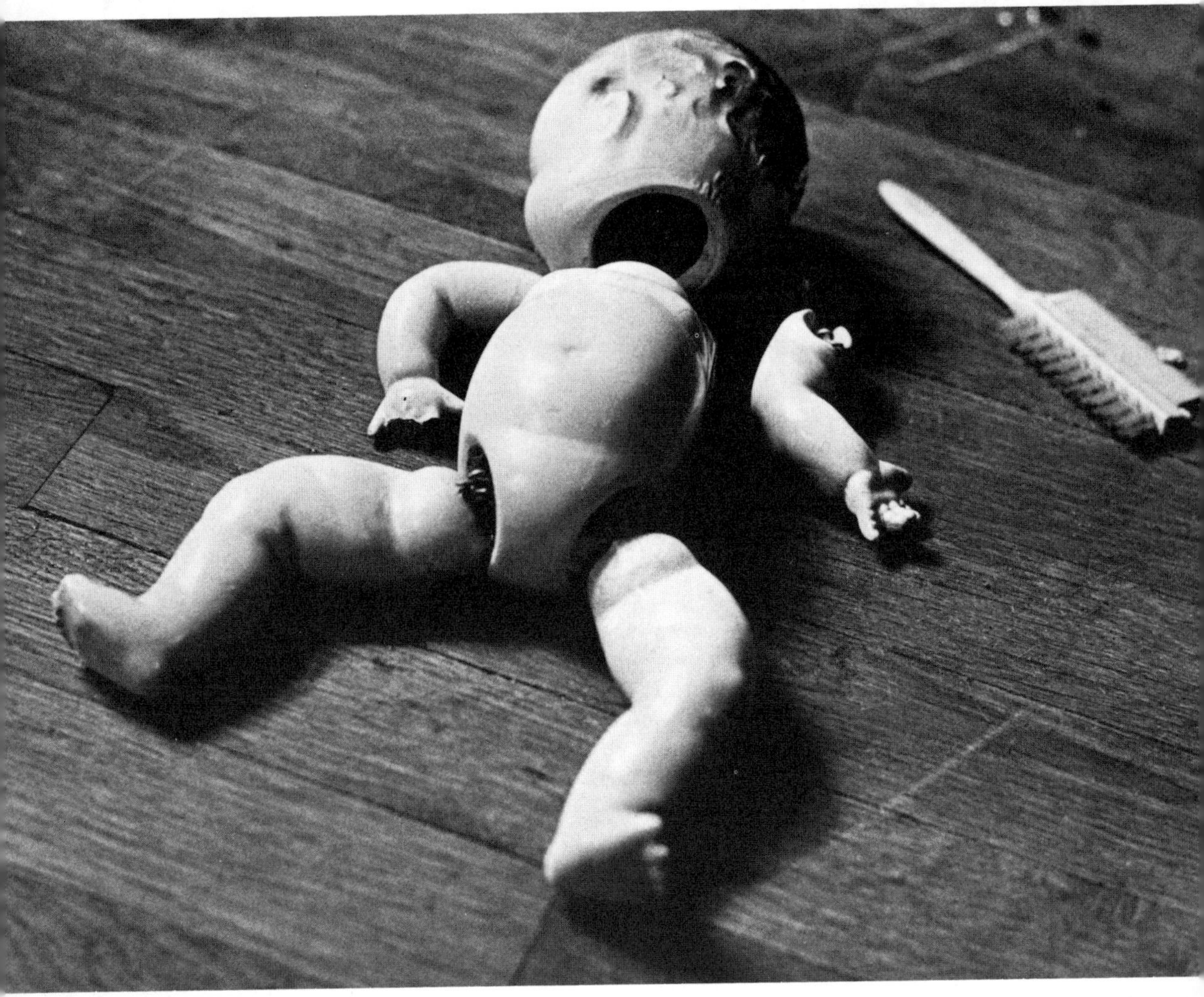

but they are very important in that they reflect *who* he is and what he is discovering.

The creativity experts point to what they call "the fourth grade slump." This is when there is a noticeable decline in spontaneity and delight. Part of the reason may be the school environment; part may be the particular cycle of growth which the child is undergoing; perhaps part of it stems from a lack of encouragement of his creative powers by parents or teachers. Whatever the cause, some of this slump can be alleviated by an awareness of it and by working to foster the child's use and development of his abilities.

When the child is sensitive to what he is experiencing, he wants to express this, and the medium of expression for him is drawing, whether that be with crayons or some paint.

Drawing serves as an outlet of expression of what is happening to the child and is something he may spend many hours doing with the smallest bit of encouragement. Some interesting insights can come from observing the artistic activities of children. One such is the following. While I was visiting the home of Mary and Karen, they were showing me the paper dolls which they themselves had made and for which they had also spent time designing clothes. One doll in particular seemed special to them; it was named Ruthie and they explained that they had made Ruthie "ugly" because they hadn't liked her very much one day. They showed me some of the clothes they had made and went to great detail about the ones designated for Ruthie. Because Ruthie seemed so important and really a part of their lives, I finally said, "Who is Ruthie?" Their answer: "Mother." By expressing their feelings of anger at their mother in their drawings, they were able to view it objectively and get it out of themselves and even laugh about it. They then showed me a dress which was Ruthie's prettiest one, because they weren't "mad at her anymore."

PLAYING DRESS-UP

Dramatization is one of the most natural and important forms of expression for the child. Acting out his feelings and ideas is part and parcel of growing up. It is a means of his gaining insights which simply cannot come any other way. Parents need not tell children to play dress-up; they only need to help children do it with ease.

The purpose of such play is not performance but rather a making clear and intensifying certain insights. Gestures too are natural forms of expression but usually by the time the child is eight or nine, he learns to inhibit much of his natural and spontaneous gesture-making. Gestures and acting can be forms of prayer if children are helped to use these in such manner. Adults' attitudes in this area are formative and can "make or break" the situation.

Dancing, singing, art work, physical exercise —any form of spontaneous action helps the person develop all of his powers. Thus encouragement of any of these expressions helps the child intensify and sharpen his possibilities as a human being. The joyful manifestation of life via dance or song or any art form is something to be hoped for and encouraged.

A child learns most when he is playing actively and involvedly. Dress-up or any form of dramatization is possibly the most dramatic and possibly the most meaningful form of learning for the child.

Watch your child playing out the drama of

his everyday life. You know from listening to him what kind of ideas he has about family life, about school, about the kind of person his father is, the kind of person he himself is. Playing school or house is the media by which the child expresses how he perceives his life in these environments and how he perceives other persons. It is the means by which he "verbalizes" what life means to him at this point in his growth and development.

Through imagination a child learns to be involved in life; he relives the events of yesterday and projects what will happen tomorrow. He prepares himself for life by reliving through play-acting what he knows about it from his knowledge of how his parents, his peers—all the persons he knows—act.

This type of play is a practice for reality for the child; it is completely serious for him and is the way he rehearses and tests his abilities for what he sees as his future. Children spend a great deal of time imitating others. Little boys learn to walk like their dads; little girls wear dresses like mom. As they grow older, they imitate other heroes and children their own age. In time, they come to develop their own modes of action, their own powers and strengths, their own ways of relating. They come to know not only their world but also themselves and who they are. Play, dress-up, any form of dramatization is their way of "testing out what is their own life-expression."

Research today is making use of this medium of play/games in order to devise "learning games" not only for children but for adults as well. Simulation is considered one of the most effective media of education and all sorts of games are being tested for their effectiveness as learning tools. The premise for this is that you learn what you do. Certainly, in the realm of childhood, play-acting is the child's learning tool.

A variation of the dramatization process is the use of puppets. Puppets have great appeal and can be used in many ways, especially in the family. Mary and Karen are very proud of the unusual puppets their family keep in a treasured place. These particular puppets were brought back from Indonesia by their older brother and are a part of the religious heritage of that nation. Puppets can be used for so many activities: story-telling, story-making-up, a family picnic, the celebration of any particular event. Children delight in performing for others, whether it be with puppets or by a talent show or any type of program.

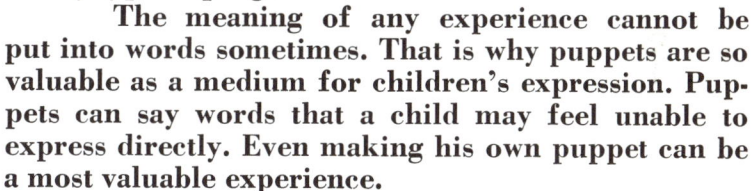

The meaning of any experience cannot be put into words sometimes. That is why puppets are so valuable as a medium for children's expression. Puppets can say words that a child may feel unable to express directly. Even making his own puppet can be a most valuable experience.

Dance has been called the most primitive expression of man's emotions. In early times there was sacred dance; David is reputed to have danced before the Lord and the legend of the juggler of our Lady is a medieval sign of its acceptance in pious circles. Dance is the most spontaneous outlet of how we really feel. Zorba typifies the person who knows how to express his feeling in a strong forceful way.

All of these forms of expressive outlets are important for the child. Parents can help their children grow in appreciation of such by making available such things as lessons in dance or music, it is true. But more important than the lessons, I think, is the encouragement to be expressive as a person. This is the task of the adult: to provide the child with time and place and the freedom to play easily and spontaneously.

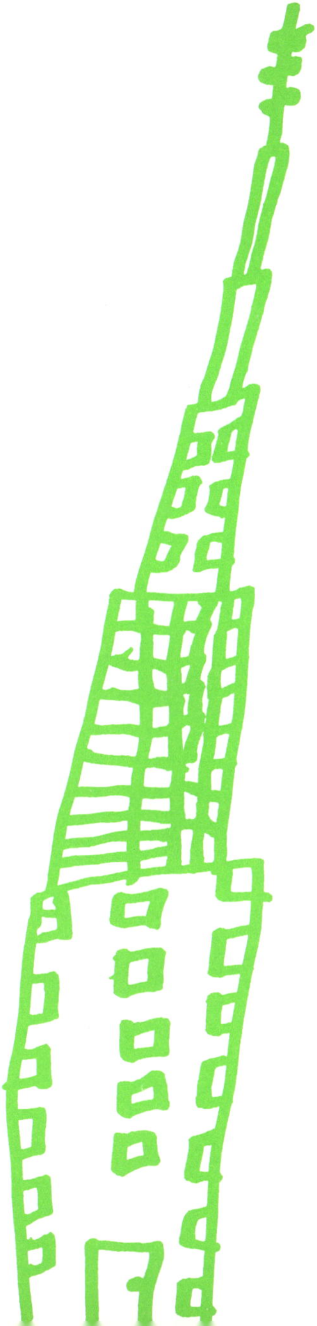

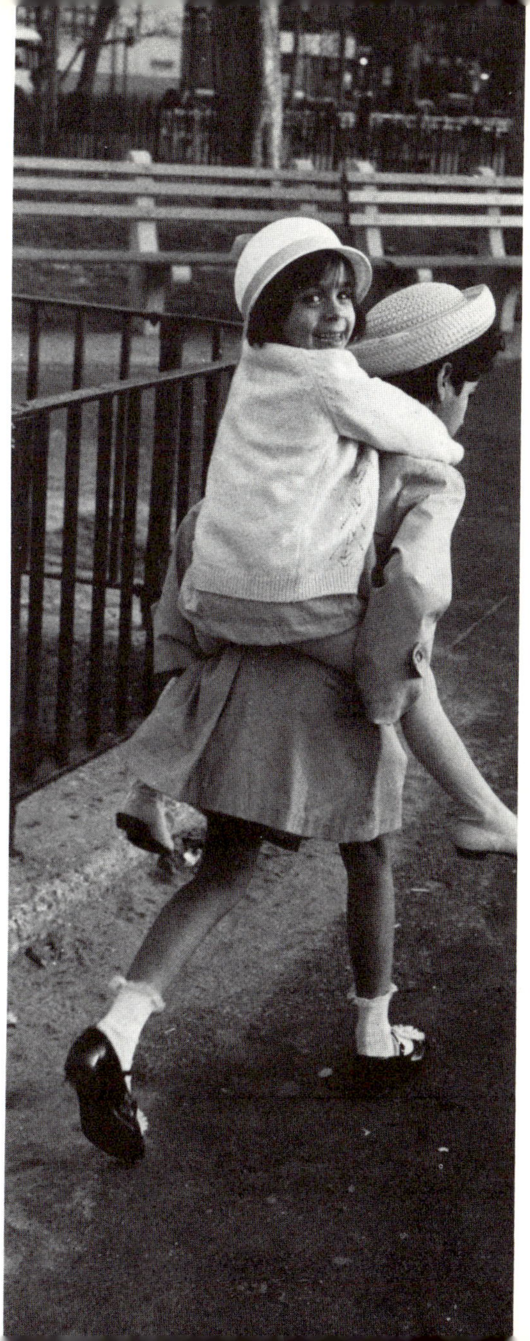

Projects in Delight

One way to help children develop their powers of expression is to encourage writing. This may seem difficult in a home situation but it is possible and highly desirable.

A family notebook, letters to grandparents or others, reading poetry and good books together are possible ways of learning to express oneself in a literary form. And the written expression of one's thoughts can be a most satisfying outlet of one's ideas.

Children can learn to write in a really exciting way if they are simply encouraged and exposed to good writing. A few years ago I helped children in a grade school put out their own literary magazine. Not only was the writing good but, more importantly, the enthusiasm and delight of the children made their venture one that was worthwhile and meaningful for them personally.

A few examples of how well children can write with just a bit of encouragement follow:

4th grade boy: "The squirrels scattered up and down the tree."
GEOFFREY STANDINGBEAR

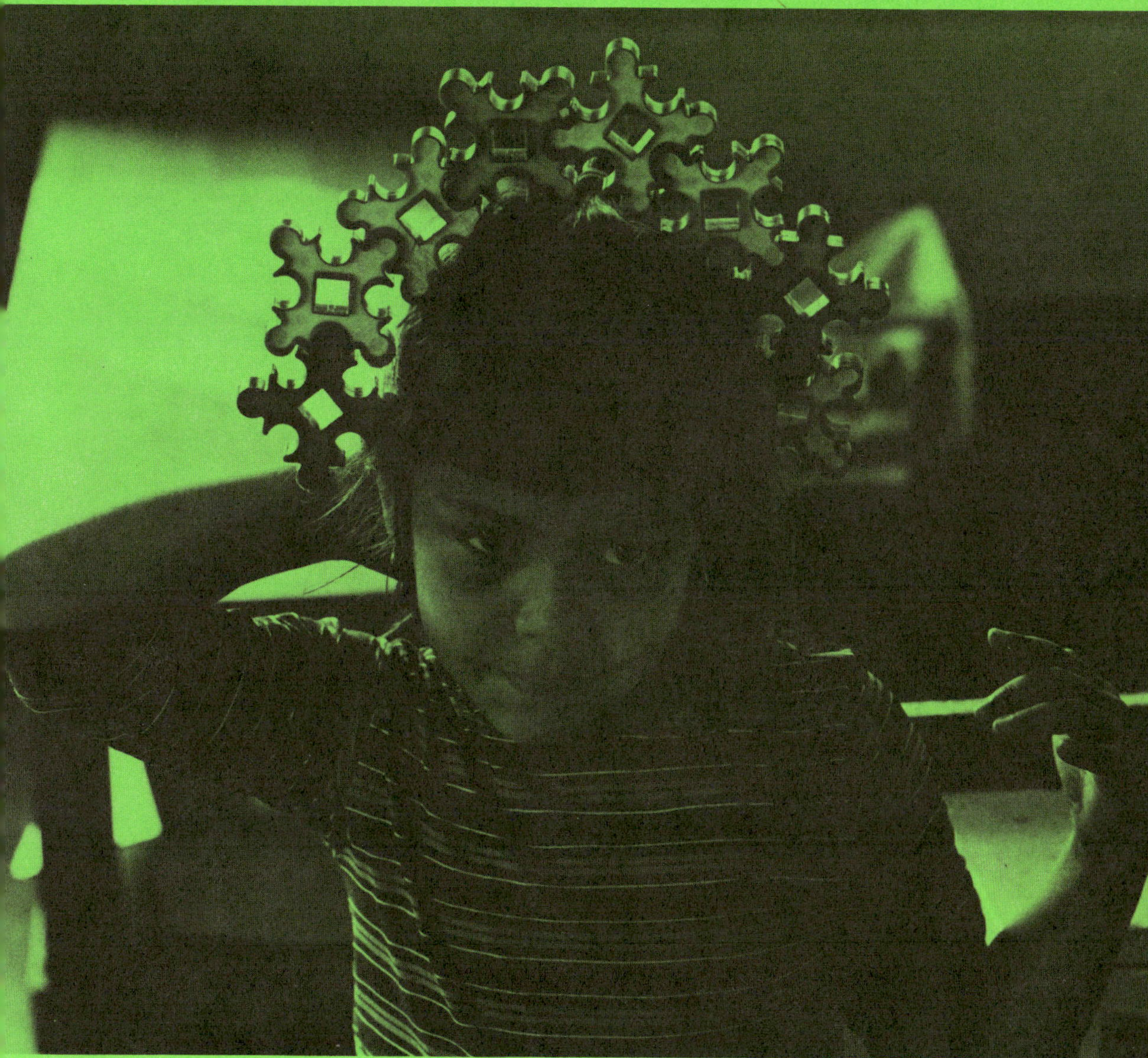

3rd grade boy: "I like to watch the skipping leaves
Roll along the ground
And hide from me."

4th grade girl: "Autumn is the time of year
when leaves leave town."

2nd grade boy: "A turtle can sleep in the water.
And he sleeps and sleeps and sleeps."

2nd grade girl: "Rain on the houses,
Rain on the trees,
Rain on my umbrella
But not on me."

6th grade boy: "The rake brushed its teeth with grass."

"The bright morning sun on the pear leaves
Sets the tree in a golden ball."

6th grade girl: "Honking geese, winging swiftly
Through the night
Play follow the leader
In the moonlight."

Children's writing reveals insight and humor as evidenced in these poems about home life:

Mud in the eyes of a four-year old girl is a kitchen.
(4th grade boy)

Beds freshly made,
Clothes on hangers,
Dust on the rag,
Dirt in the sweeper:
Allowance Day.
      ANAMARIE MOYNIHAN

Find wetness, mud-berry pies
   plus a bath-beckoning body
And you've got a product,
   namely a child
With subdivisions of snoring,
   kid sister and hard-hitting brothers.
How can we grownups cling to the hope
   that they will soon grow up?
                JANE HUSTEN

The clinking of silver
The shatter of plates
Then the bang of the door—
The dishes are done.
      MARTY LEROUX

by 8th graders

Children delight in nature and, if encouraged, come up with delightful word-pictures:

Trees
cast silhouettes
of long scrawny fingers
in black against
the golden disc
of autumn moon.
      (8th grade girl)

A bush of tea roses,
White iron chairs on a velvet lawn,
Sunlight falling upon mellow silverware
and old mahogany,
Dark tree shapes against a mauve sky—
Pin points of a summer afternoon.
      (8th grade girl)

The clouds huddling,
The beating of lightning,
The agony of the wind
Make a spring rain.
The sound of crickets,
The weather-beaten earth,
The trees combing the sky
Make a spring night.
This is the splitting of the seasons,
The slash of spring.
    KATIE SHAW (6th grade girl)

Folding mountains
with rigid sides
let scurrying waters
jag down a waterfall.
   (8th grade girl)

Barefoot blossoms
peek out
from a still-brown
 hillside.
  CHERE SUBLETT
  (8th grade girl)

Hushed hills
 abandoned homespun suits
 and feasted
 on dogwood and redbud.
   MARTY LEROUX
   (8th grade girl)

Pink-toed apple blossoms
 thunder the arrival of spring
 then fade into songs of summer.
  JERRY McGRANN (6th grade boy)

If the child is encouraged to write such observations about nature and his life on a routine basis, he will also come to write with depth about his feelings.

Being able to express feelings through writing—and especially good writing—is of highest importance for the young person. It gives him a great deal of satisfaction to put down on paper exactly how he feels and this written expression serves as an outlet for his emotions.

Some examples of such reflections by thirteen-year-olds follow:

> I am unique. Only I could have desk and surroundings looking like a hurricane had burrowed through. Only I could trip over the doorway. Only I could fall UP the stairs. Only I could stumble over the ball in dribbling. I want to be different, famous because I'm me, but I'm caught in a net of mediocrity. I want to be original, but to do so would be to break away from the gang. To live in social isolation is usually the fate of the original. I don't know if I want to pay that price or not. I want to be unique, all right. Unique like everybody else.
>
> PADDY DONOVAN

> If you looked at me you would see many things: a small, blonde-haired, blue-eyed girl, a student scurrying in and out among books. Or you might see a teenager with four younger brothers. After breakfast you would see me as one of the thousands who use Colgate, or in school as a blue

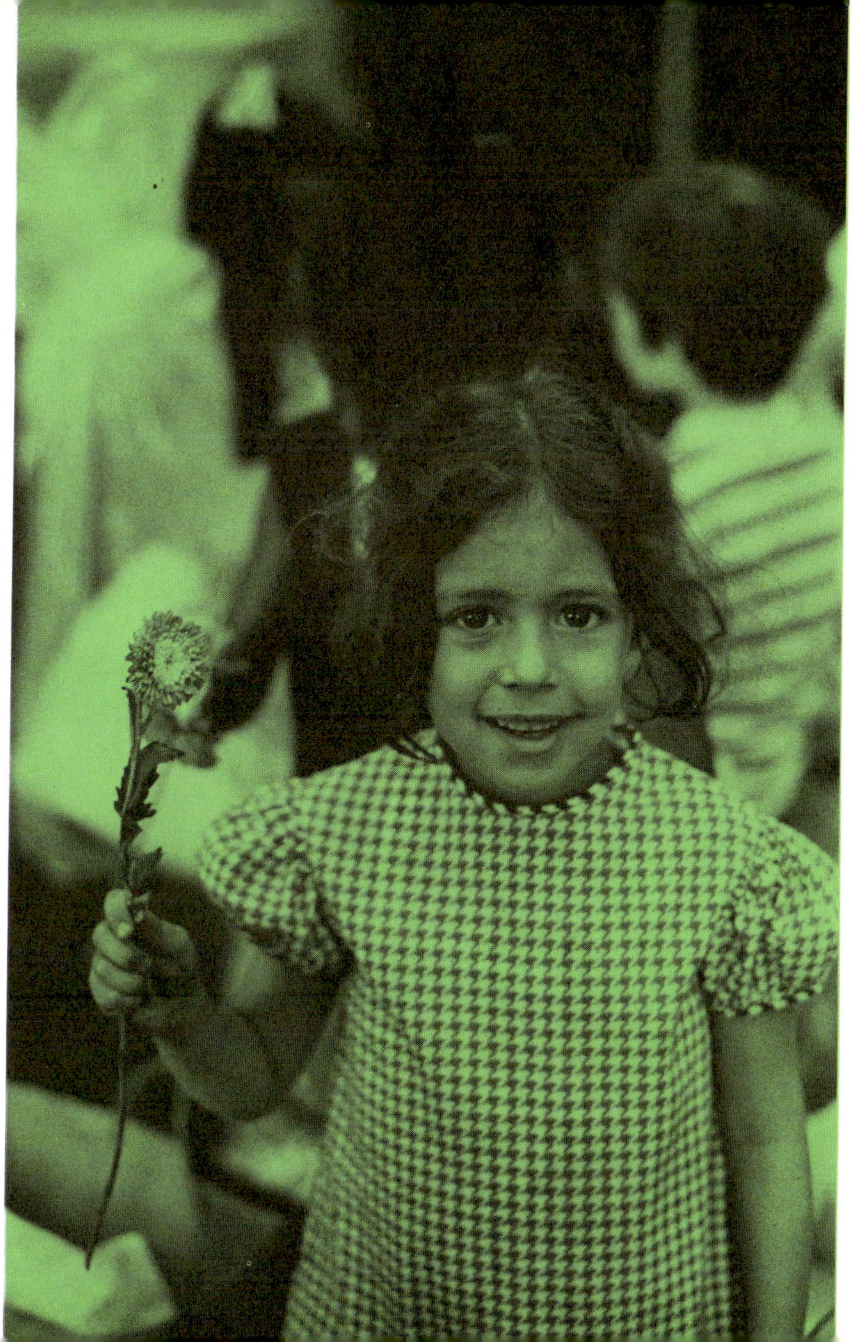

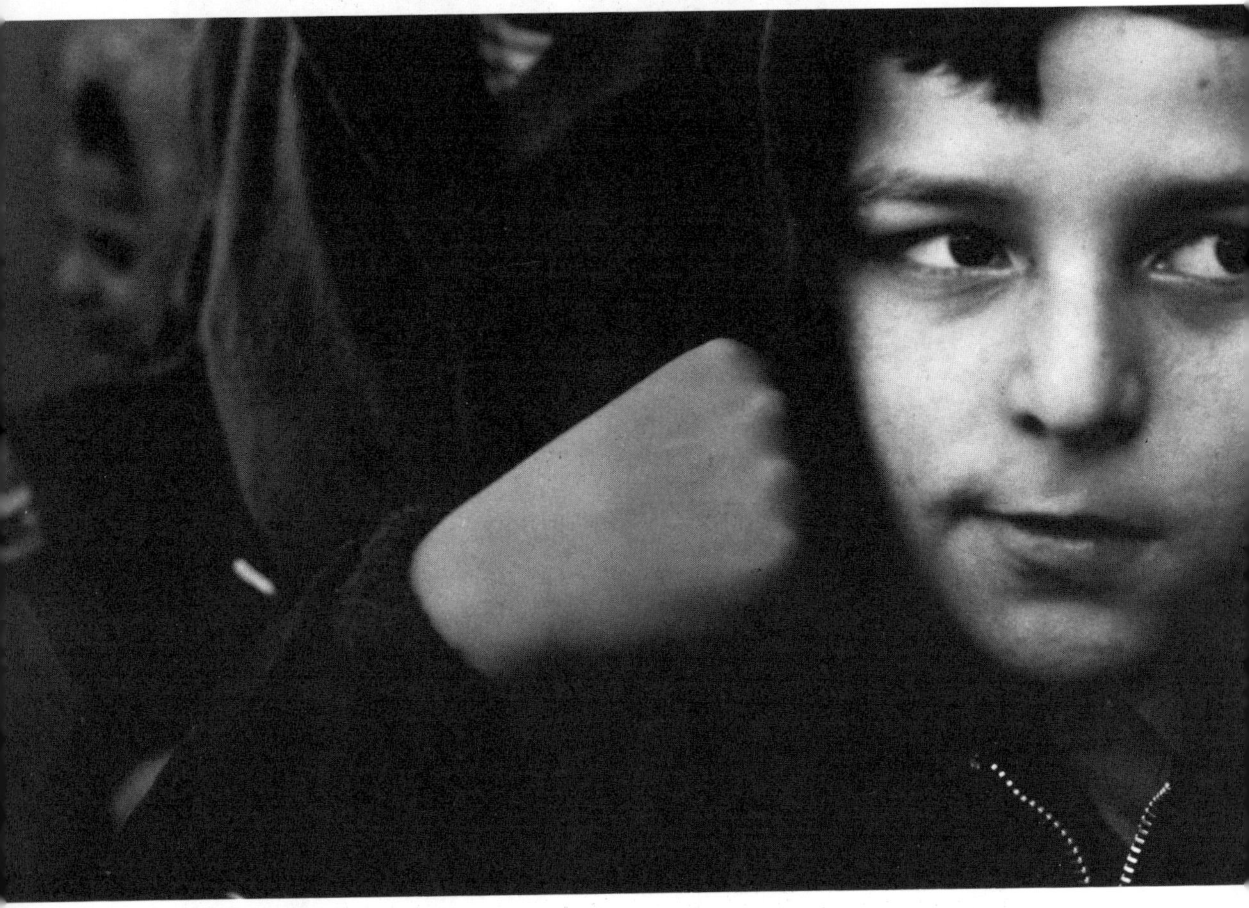

and white uniform. But if you could look inside me while I am in different moods, you might find several things: A nobody treading on the cobblestones of life; '$&*!)& (Secret Agent, Expert in Codes in Ciphering) or maybe a telepath exploring the stars. No matter where you look, inside and out, in my school work or my room, you will find **me.**

SARA MATHIAS

Green-gray eyes in a rather palish face, blonde fly-away hair and a lanky body draped elegantly (like a rag doll) over a stuffed chair munching apples, sipping ginger ale. Regardez-vousing a book of French or spinnin' round Saturn encased in a tale of science fiction; stumbling through an obstacle course of Liszt or tripping through dancing class: THIS is me.

FRANCES SMITH

Who am I really? Am I just a name in a roster that someone skims over and never really notices? Or am I a separate personality, different from those other names? How am I different? I'm me! And there's no one else like me in the whole world. No one with the same thoughts and solutions. Great, isn't it? And a little frightening too. But that means I've got to work extra hard. The world is only going to know one me. I want them to remember.

ERIN DONOVAN

Who am I in a world of wars and rockets where no one cares what happens to anyone else? I live in a world of joy, fear, laughter and sorrow. Where do I fit in?
      Who am I in a world of rockets and wars, where no one cares what happens to anyone? where people are treated like dirt, and freedom is taken for granted? Who am I but one of the millions of greedy people constantly wanting more and never happy with what I have . . . who am I?
                              EILEEN BRYCE

I felt my spirit
   hushed against stone
and I bowed my head
  in the cold crust
  of my shadow.
          KIPPY CAMERON

The ashes of loneliness
burnt and black
floated into the world
to populate the ruins of despair
but from the coffin of destruction
emerges the tick-tock balance
of happiness in my heart
for
I only remember
a joy-streaked life
and love poured into forms
of family.
I only remember time gone by
and love spent on days
woven with happiness.
                  CHERE SUBLETT

Religious feelings seem to resound more with the feeling of gratitude than anything else and this after all is a rather sound basis for faith and for rejoicing in the gift of life:

When you wander down streets and lanes
and the filth and ignorance of your town-mates
       surrounds you,
you see the desperate hope
that is the only hope against discrimination.
You see the faith and belief in better times ahead
that will never be satisfied.

And you hear the prayer to God for help
and you realize that it is to the same God
whom you worship in immaculate chapels.

Then if you let these people help you
by your helping them,
prisons walls collapse,
and hostages find themselves free.
The spring is eternal
and April rains are fragrant
and bands of beauty last forever.
Then you know
that through your gift of yourself
the Kingdom of God is among your kind.
                              BETH CHERRY

God's kingdom is a crowd at a baseball game,
the Coke friends share after the game
and the party celebrating the victory.
God's kingdom is the smell of pine trees

      after the rain
or the feeling of walking in the sand.
God's kingdom is you—where you go
      and what you do.
KATIE SHAW

Who makes light?
The pastel velvet petals of a flower?
The silk-laced wings of a butterfly?
The feather-pressed gown of birds?
Who gives the entrance of a new life?
A sprig of grass?
An April shower?
God creates each precious hour.
CINDY PHILLIPS

It's the little things I thank you for:
the orange stillness of the dawn,
the pink and gold of a setting sun,
and geese flying past a harvest moon,
the smell of rain beating down,
wind blowing through my hair
and balls of dew on velvet blades of grass.
These are the tiny things I love so much.
MARY ORTHWEIN

And from a fifth grader:

Flowers in broad daylight rising with the sun,
Rose and ivory honey-suckles coaxing bees to hum,
Laughing golden daffodils catching morning dew,
Dangling in the crisp spring breeze,
Whimpering all day through,

Pink-powdered rose buds dancing in the air,
God made these things just for me
And planted them with care.

KATHY SCHERER

Sylvia Ashton-Warner in her now classic *Teacher* points to the importance of such self-expression. In her work with the Maori children, she relied heavily on using their own language in the school situation and had the children make their own books.

"I try to bring as many facets of teaching into the creative vent as possible, with emphasis on reading and writing. And that's just what organic teaching is: all subjects in the creative vent. It is just as easy for a teacher, who gives a child a brush and lets him paint, to give him a pencil and let him write, and to let him pass his story to the next one to read. Simplicity is so safe. There is no occasion whatever for the early imposition of a dead reading, a dead vocabulary. It is like a frame over a young tree making it grow in an unnatural shape."

Something she says about the New Zealand society applies equally well to our own today:

"Seldom have they had to reach inward to grasp the thing that they wanted. Everything, from material requirements to ideas, is available ready-made. From mechanical gadgets to sensation in the films they can buy almost anything they fancy. They can buy life itself from the film and radio—canned life. And even if they tried to reach inward for something that maybe they couldn't find manufactured, they would no longer find anything there.

They've dried up. From babyhood they have had shiny toys put in their hands, and in the kindergartens and infant rooms bright pictures and gay material. Why conceive anything of their own? There has not been the need. The capacity to do so has atrophied and now there is nothing there. The vast expanses of the mind that could have been alive with creative activity are now no more than empty vaults that must, for comfort's sake, be filled with non-stop radio, and their conversation consists of a list of platitudes and cliches."

And her most important message, I think, is that creativity in these formative years is the solution to war, that destructiveness and creativity stem from the same vent and creativity is the solution to such capacity for destruction.

A more recent effort along somewhat the same lines is *The Me Nobody Knows* (Children's Voices from the Ghetto) which was edited by Stephen M. Joseph. The whole enterprise was devoted to publishing the writing of children. If there is a strong writing program in the school, children will be writing at home naturally. If there is not, home encouragement may foster the development of another kind of creative force in persons.

Along somewhat the same order I think one of the most important sharing times between parents and children is reading together. There are so many books that are truly children's classics. Not only is this a sharing for parents and children and thus a building of communication, but from the standpoint of exposure to good literature, it is important.

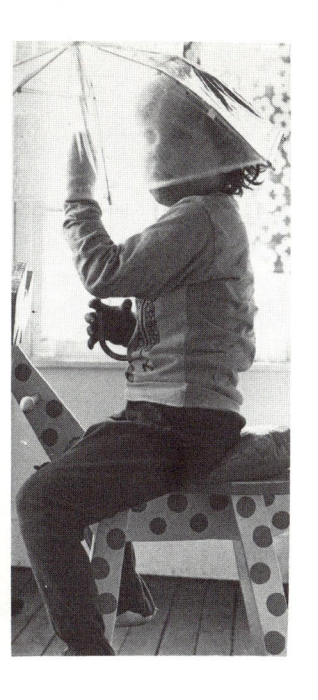

Books like *Swimmy, Buttons in the Back, Charlotte's Web, One Hundred Dresses, Hailstones and Halibut Bones, The Giving Tree, The Velveteen Rabbit, The Little Prince* as well as many, many others have important messages both for growing-up and grown-up. It is an often forgotten truth that the best children's books are really adult.

Watching television or movies together and a mutual sharing of ideas about what has been seen by parents and children is a valuable thing to do. It is estimated that children watch 15,000 hours of television by the time they graduate from high school, most of it without any type of evaluative process or any help in learning to be selective. Norms of evaluation are badly needed so that children do not just absorb everything in toto they view.

A program which has received high praise for its appeal and educational value for children is "Sesame Street." There are parent-teaching guides available for this excellent new use of the television media. Another program highly recommended by everything I have read is "Misteroger's Neighborhood." Consult your local television station for information and listings.

What We Want for Our Children

Today's children are children of television. Today's children are at home in New York, London, Biafra, and Vietnam. They are familiar with the moon; they know hippies and California by sight and spend hours absorbed in swift-moving, violent dramas. For them television seems life and the reality of life itself is rather boring by comparison.

Religion must be a part of their world just as television or any other reality is. Forms of faith must be such that the young person can understand them, can see them as integral to their own life-style and can joyfully consider them as a part of the future adulthood.

The characteristics of our time—technology, mobility, freedom, personalism, questioning, honesty, a deep involvement in all the issues of our times—are taken for granted by our children. If a deeply engrained Christian perspective is part of their attitude in all of these areas, it must be part and parcel of their formation in the home and environment of growth.

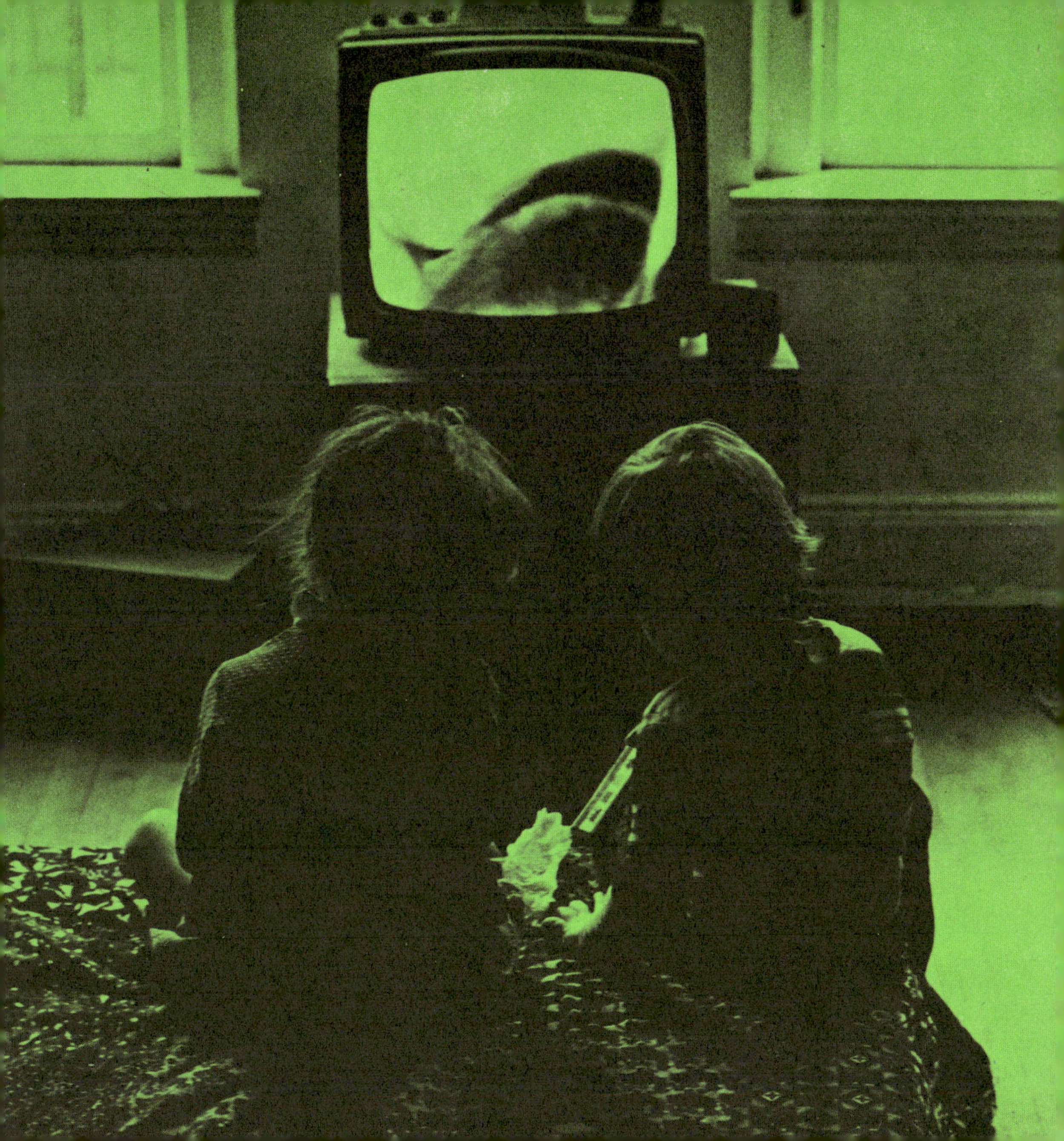

Parents teach love by loving, giftedness by giving and sharing, happiness by deeply nurtured habits of life-loving, openness by their acceptance of others. Home is where a child learns that he is loved, that life is to be shared and given, that he is a good person, that his family cares about him and all of life, and because of this experience he grows in believing there is a Creator of such good things as life and love.

It is through life shared in the family that the child discovers who God is and what kind of God he is. The factors which help young people choose faith are adults who understand them, freedom in which to choose, a community of believers and an image of God as someone who loves them.

Gabriel Moran has said, "What those growing up so desperately need is a human being who will take them from where they are, who will believe in them to such an extent that they also will come to believe, who will hold on with an adult love that will never overwhelm but will never let go. Whatever teachers or parents communicate to children, above all they communicate the loves which dominate their lives. You influence most of all by what you love."

Haim Ginnott says something of the same thing when he says that it is by indicating our sympathy and understanding of the child that we show that we love them. A child's feelings must always be taken seriously and if the problem cannot be solved as often it cannot (his puppy was run over, he missed six problems in math, his best friend is moving away), he can be soothed and comforted by expressions of concern and understanding from his parents.

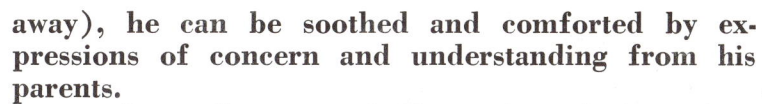

Just telling our children about faith or love is not enough. What is more important is how we feel about our faith or how we feel about loving our children. It is how we live what we say we love and believe that is the acid test and witnesses to our children the reality of it all.

Our children do not expect us to give them answers so much as they expect us to live what we say we believe. Today's children live in a worldwide environment in which they are involved in every kind of human situation. Information is at their fingertips and our task is not so much to give them knowledge as to help them acquire standards of value by which they can evaluate what they are perceiving. Again, it is a matter of our attitudes which will be the influential factor in determining the quality of life our children absorb. Our attitudes in the home or classroom are the atmosphere, are the learning situation.

We want to teach our children that life is good. They can only live life meaningfully, Christianly, hopefully, if they believe this. They can only celebrate it if they see that life is a joyful gift. Our own attitudes are the most fundamental medium of saying that life is a gift. Our own ability to celebrate in a joyful way is the most direct way of affirming our faith in life and a loving God.

Joy is not a pollyanna attitude or a lack of realistic practical-ness. Rather, it is a deep underly-

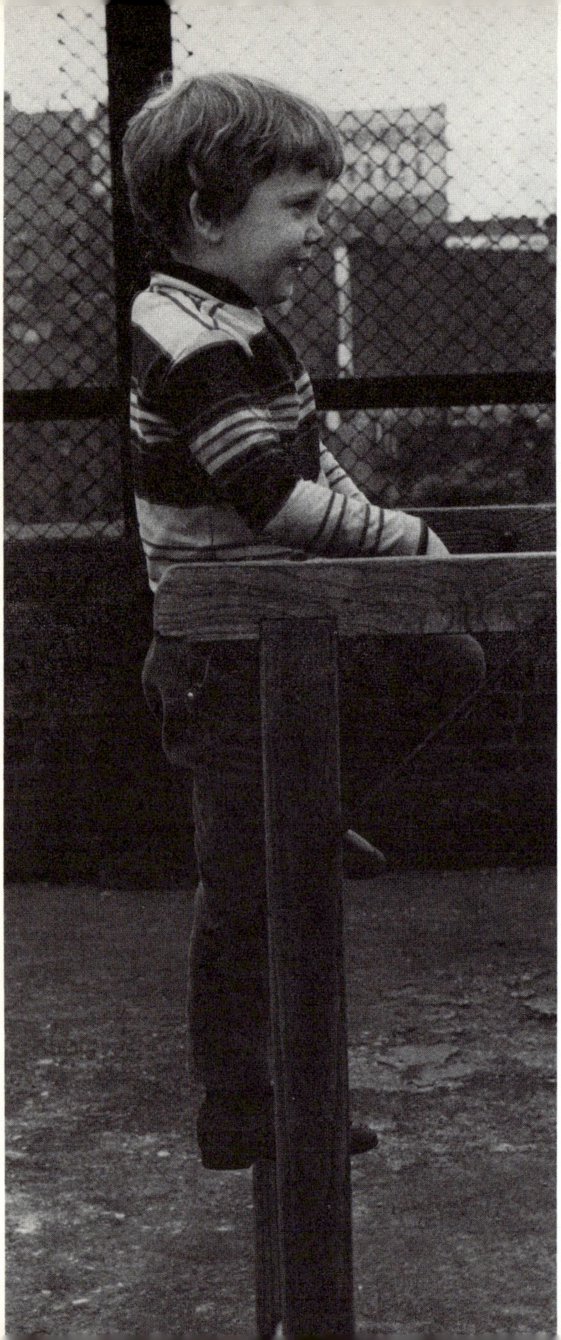

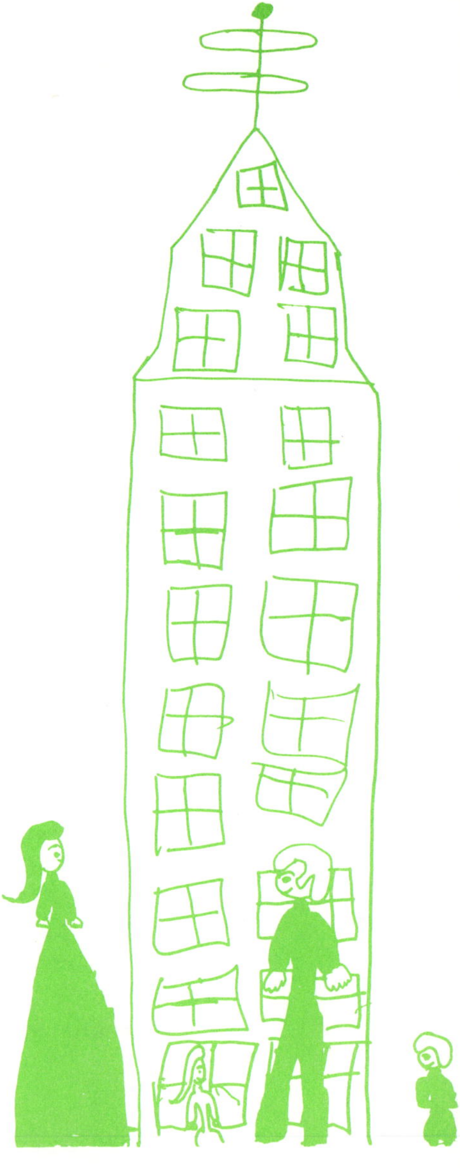

ing affirmation that despite pain and hardship, despite the sacrifices one must sometimes make, despite suffering and whatever kind of particular wear and tear is present for this particular family, despite all of this, life has meaning and purpose, life is mostly gift, life is to be shared and it is for loving, for giving. This atmosphere permeates a home and makes the mornings sing, the tone in the air warm and cheerful, makes upheavals bearable, makes the family a loving place to be.

Haim Ginnott says communication is the key to settling the undeclared wars which often leave both parent and child, angry, confused, hurt. He makes the premise that life should be considered a dance rather than a game. In a game there must be a winner and thus a loser. Cooperation, movement, rhythm mark the operation of a dance. You are partners, not competitors.

Talking with children has rules and meanings that are proper to this particular kind of conversation. A child should be taken seriously. Even as adults, we cannot think about world problems if we are unable to cope with a particular situation at hand. When <u>we feel understood</u> by another, we feel loved. Thus, to understand that a child's stomach hurts or that he feels bad because he lost a toy or that he quarreled with a friend is to help him feel loved. The barrier that rises between parents and children is so tragic because there is not a lack of love between the two but there is a lack of respect for the other and for the other's feelings.

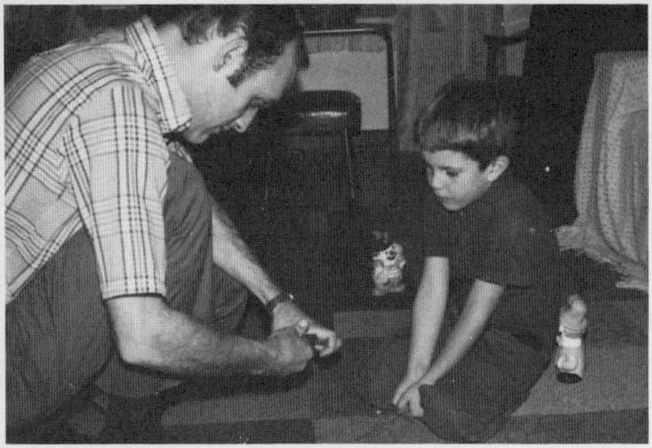

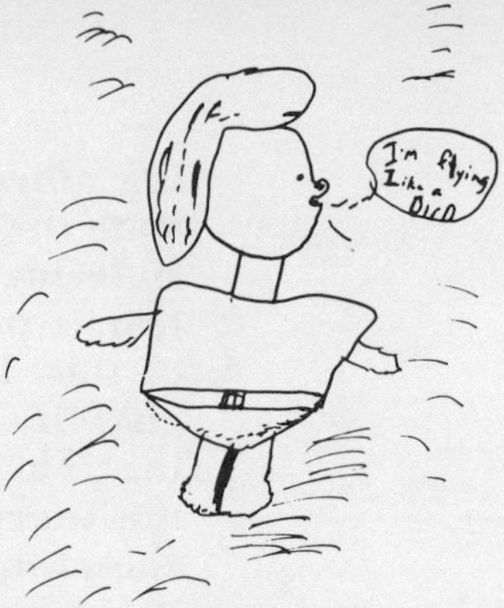
I'm flying Like a DicD

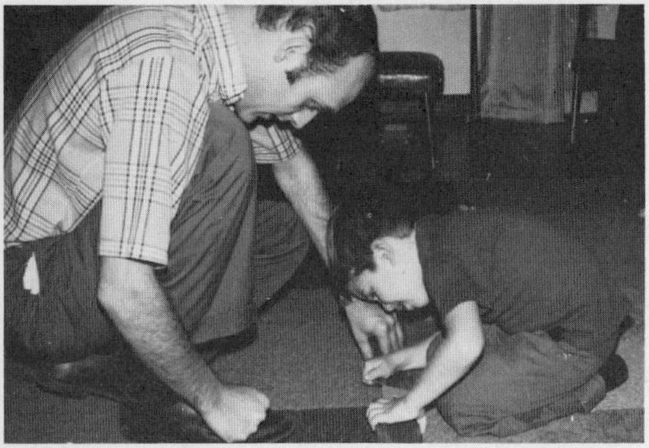

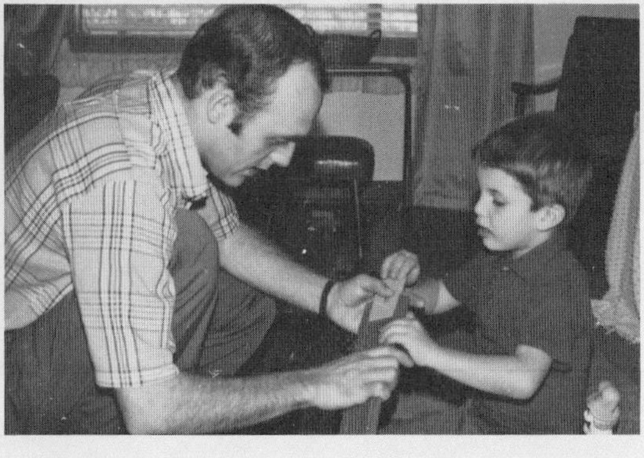

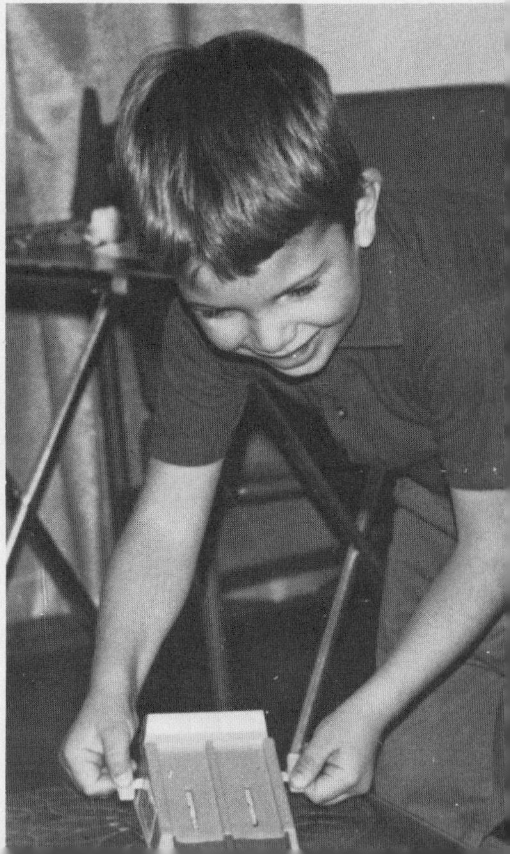

discipline

Discipline is part and parcel of growth. It seems the most important thing is that parents and children both know who is boss and both know that there is love involved in whatever happens. One of the most important qualities and at the same time most difficult to achieve is that of consistency in maintaining discipline. Parents and teachers are humans with headaches, problems, worries, with tempers, moods, and all the kinds of human disorder and failure that everyone has. Children sometimes expect parents to be perfect; parents sometimes expect children to be perfect. There has to be a mutual understanding about the fact that neither is.

Haim Ginnott has been quoted but he is not the answer for everyone. Your own sense of fairness, of love, of what is best for your children and your home life is the key to how you handle problems that are the inevitable part of every family. It is the fact of your love which will make bearable whatever pain is involved in helping children grow through difficult times and situations.

honesty

My personal opinion is that honesty by parents is probably one of the most important qualities that can be a part of the shared family life. Children will imitate whatever attitudes you have; they will respect honesty, whether it has to do with why they are being punished or why there are problems in the world. Tact, gentleness, love are all part of this honest dimension, however, and temper the kind of frankness you display.

Parents and teachers today have a tremendous task in helping children grow up. The old standards sometimes seem rather inadequate but the basis of these standards—love, concern, honesty, trust, communication, sharing—is still a necessary part of home life.

I don't think it very often occurs to adults to respect children. We are too prone to dismiss their ideas or feelings or see them in a context that is unrelated to life. We thus diminish their own self-esteem and harden them against openness to a lot of beauty and delight, and worst of all, we fail to establish communication with them.

If we believe education is a process of learning, we are always learning. As adults, our role is to help children explore and discover meanings and events. The power of perception lies in the person and is revealed only when the outside climate proves conducive or "safe" for such revelation. As the child sees his world, he attaches meaning to it. He views it in a highly personal, completely unique manner, and much of the learning that is taking place has to do with his interaction with the "other" and himself.

Children learn from everything they touch; they express what they learn through their actions, their play and their art forms. Adults can share in this world; they can be there to discover with the child what world, life, person, everything is about; they can continue to discover mystery in all the things they thought they knew. Children's learning takes place both in a dramatic way and in subtle ways. Sudden is everyday. All new facts bombard them and they are nearly drunk with the simple wonder that each day brings to them. However, the change which is part of the process of learning will become evident only in the long haul of their becoming adults. The process of absorbing and sifting out what is valuable will not be done except over the next few years of adolescence and young adulthood.

We thus do not need to teach our children; they are learning. What we need to do is to share that learning with them. Talk to them, with them; explore with them, delight with them, listen to them and share all that is with them.

This is not to say that a child-centered family to the exclusion of adult interests is what is being encouraged. On the contrary, a very important part of what children absorb is the love-relationship that is or isn't there between husband and wife. This growing sharing love for one another has to be the core of the family life and the children participate in it by their sensing how much daddy loves mother, how deep mother's feelings are for dad. Psychologist Henri Nouwen points to this in his book *Intimacy* when he discusses love between man and woman: "The highest safeguard for the physical, mental, and spiritual health of the child is not primarily the attention paid to the child but the unrestricted love of the parents for each other." They see, in the same way they know how they are loved, the concrete evidence of this bond: carefully ironed shirts, his favorite dish, how dad helps mom by taking out the trash or fixing the broken light fixture (if he can do such things) or other small, seemingly insignificant, gestures which speak love.

In our day and age being a parent seems a task of tremendous magnitude and anxiety can easily be the key attitude. There are no absolute ways of being parents; concern is necessary but so is a healthy realistic attitude of relaxation. Probably the key to it is balance, a hard task for anyone in any position but one which makes a vast difference in the way we approach things. Being relaxed removes a lot of problems from the situation, makes the burdens not so heavy, gives the dimension of a kind of humor to it all and somehow often puts the whole thing in its proper context.

There is just so much that any of us can do for another. We can instruct a person but we cannot force him. We can give him the tools and all that he needs but we cannot do the job for him. And that's important to remember. What we are hoping to bring about in our children is a sense of responsibility, a self-direction by which he will live all the things we want him to become. Providing a healthy atmosphere in which he will learn such goals is the extent of our thrust.

To grow in self-understanding, to be able to have deep personal relationships with other persons, to have an awareness of the world around him, to be able to assume mature responsibility for himself and others, to be able to communicate and to think:

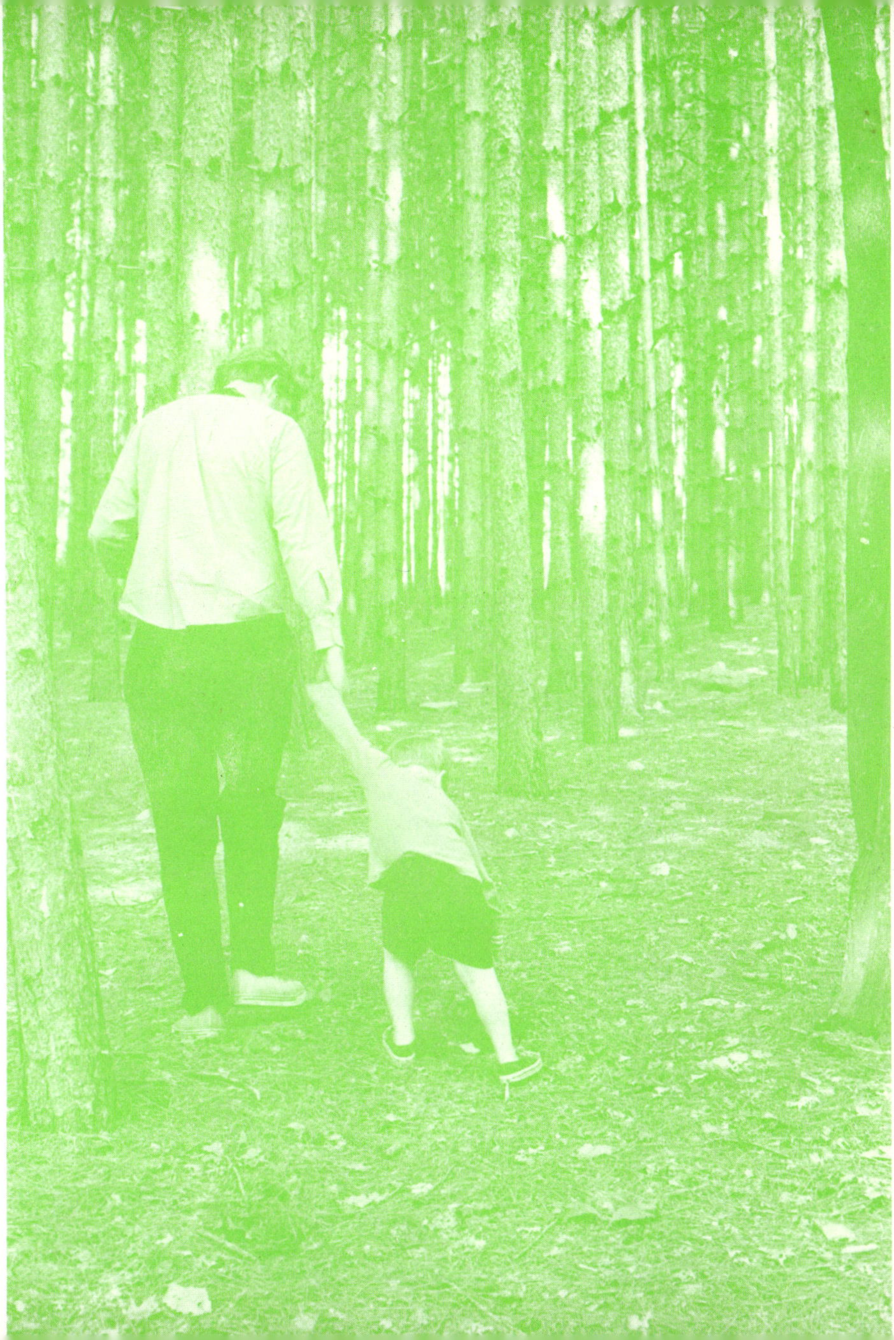

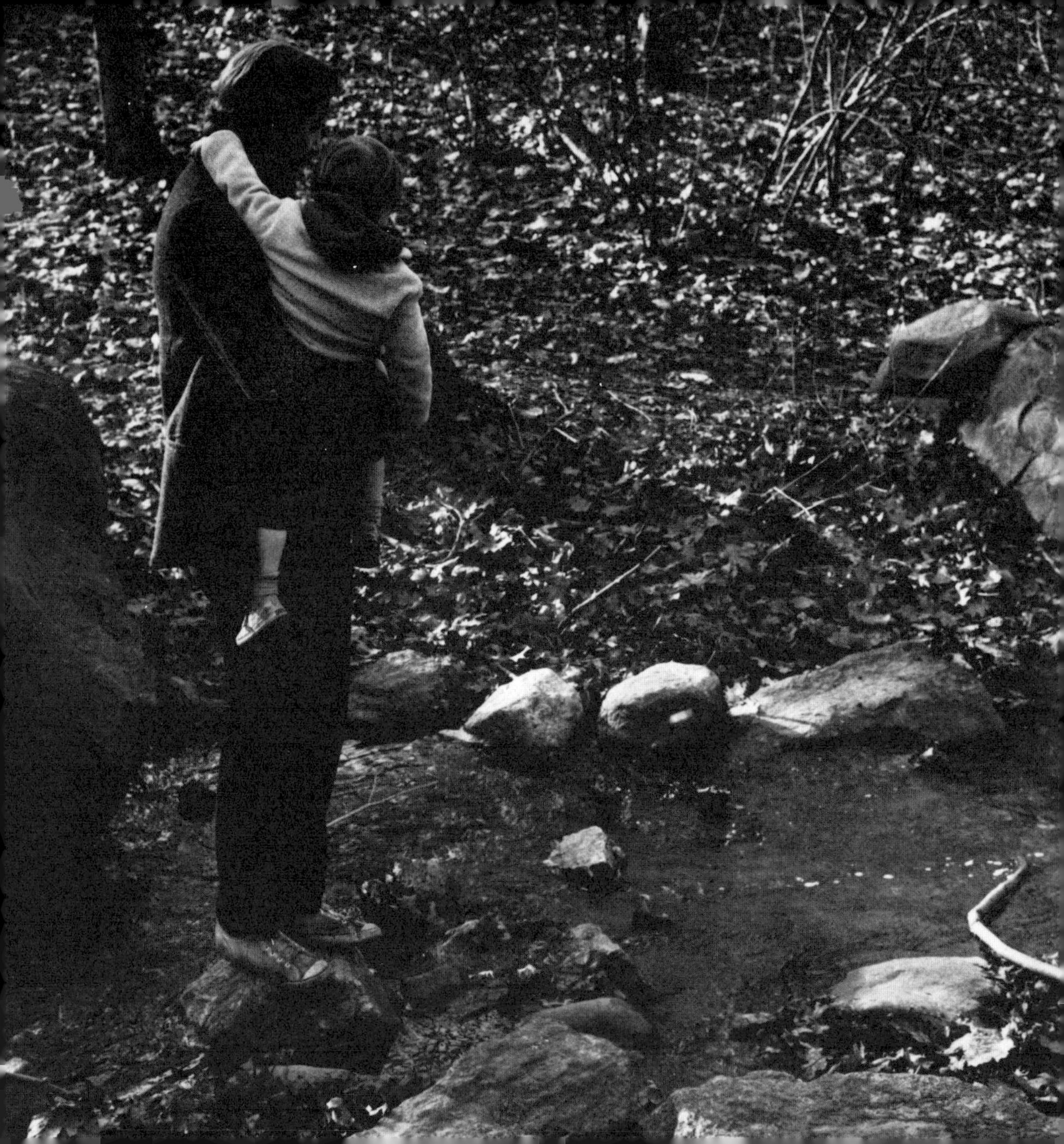

these are some of the tools we would like to give to our children. Such values will make of him a man who is a Christian, who is a meaning-maker for others, who is able to creatively renew our world and make of it a better place for all men.

Values are more than words; they must be lived out in the everyday world. Human beings learn to live fully in the larger community from their experience of the small community which begins with their own family circle. In this environment the infant acquires a sense that the world is friendly, that there is someone who cares, that he has value and is loved, that he is free to grow and learn about himself and the world. Such a preparation is the most and best each of us can give those children for whom we share responsibility. There may be no better.

Your Own Chapter

Each day is new. Each day there is something to be learned, something to be shared. This chapter is one that you and your children can write together.

Mary and Karen spent a part of the Christmas vacation painting rocks. Try doing some yourself.

Spend an extra five minutes today with each of your children. Tomorrow each of them will be a day older.

Go on a nature hike. Collect leaves or rocks or flowers or look for treasures.

Visit the zoo.

Write a family letter to grandmother.

Start a collection of leaves, spoons, owls, caps, buttons, butterflies . . .

Watch your child watch himself in the mirror.

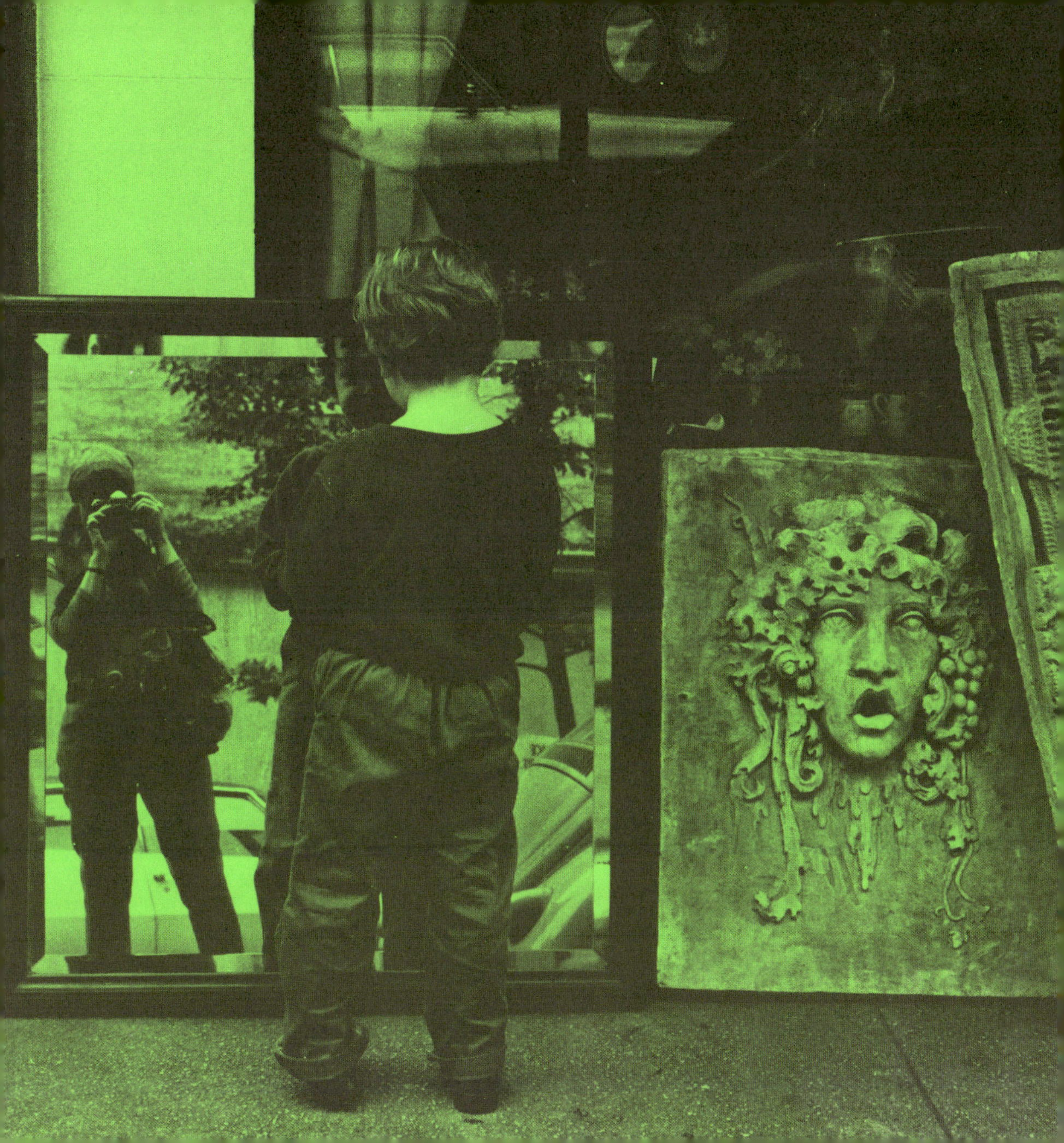

Have a treasure hunt in the park.

Forget about television tonight. See what you as a family can do: make popcorn, jigsaw puzzles, play *Monopoly*, music, or just talk.

Put up a chalkboard or bulletin board in the children's room for them to use as their own. (Corkboard, flannelboard, or burlap are good. Or use corrugated paper from an empty box.)

Make some special books that are just for indoor times. My mother made three scrapbooks which were for rainy or sick days. They were such special treasures, and they gave us a feeling of special concern because she had spent time preparing them for days when we would not be able to enjoy the usual "fun" things. The pictures were ordinary ones, but the books were quite special.

Bring each of the children something small as a surprise from the store today, just for being themselves.

Go for a drive this weekend to see the countryside, or go to the park for the afternoon.

Make up games to play in the car: how many cars, road signs, policemen, colors of cars—the possibilities are endless. Or fix a box for the children with toys in it—inexpensive ones—and maybe a cookie or cracker. Make it a surprise.

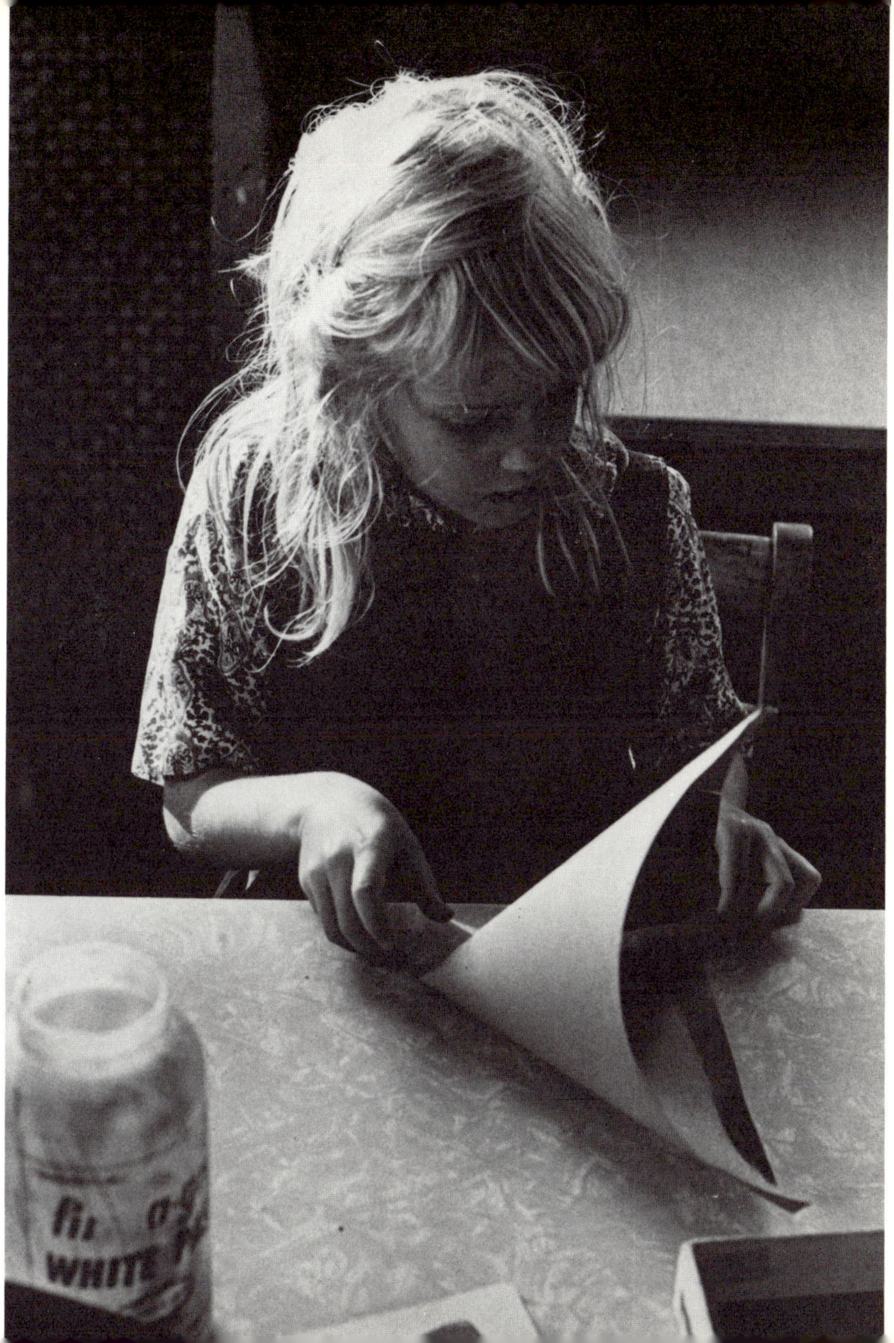
WHITE

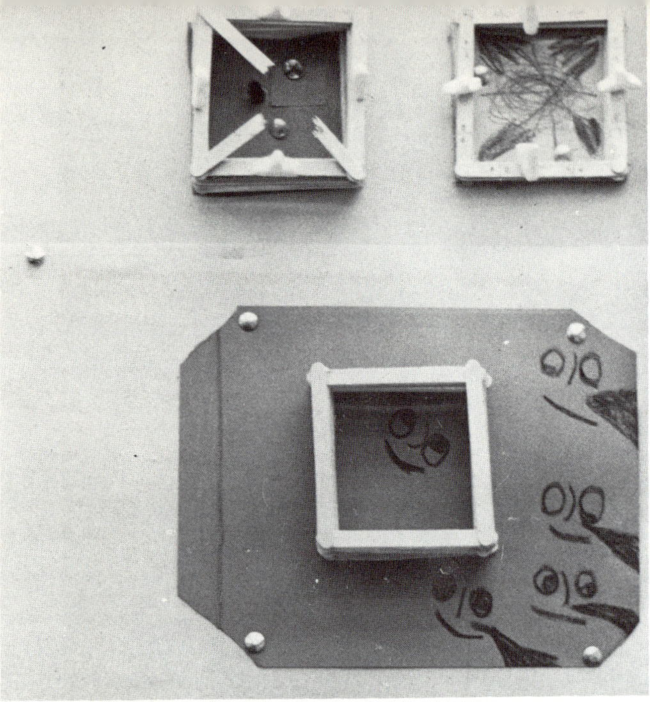

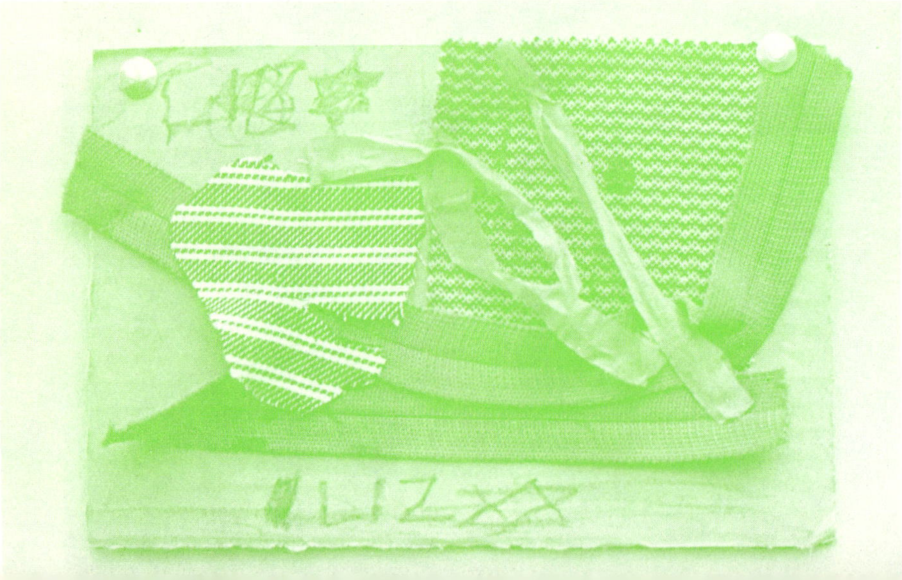
LIZ

Put some classical music on the phonograph and dance to it, or be a conductor.

Make a map of the house or the yard. Maybe a treasure map.

Bake cookies.

Look at the stars.

Have a family council. Meet once a week or less often to make family decisions: what television programs to watch, what jobs will be done by whom, how the family money will be spent.

Take time while you are peeling potatoes or helping your pre-schooler tie his shoe to play games like: How many things in this room are red? blue? green? etc.? What letters of the alphabet can you say? What are things that begin with A? etc.? Name all the grown-ups you know?

Buy velour paper (it feels like velvet) or use swatches of color from your sewing box. Cut into triangles, squares, circles, etc., and let your little ones make designs with them. Color and texture are two tools which your young children need to use often and which they never tire of playing with.

Moving things hold a special fascination for the very young. Inexpensive mobiles that are delightful—fish, owls, circles, clowns, chickens, etc.—are marvelous companions for children. You can make your own with nylon thread or coat hangers and some experimentation. Better still, help them make their own.

Make a big tree out of butcher paper; paint it with tempera or sponges or fingers or crayolas or corrugated paper. Put it on a wall where the children can sit under it, can add "leaves" such as their pictures or fingerpaints or snowflakes or whatever designs they wish.

Small children like to play with their hands; take time to do "shadow stories" with them. That's an occupation our grandparents had in an evening. It's worth doing with your little children because it gives them a sense of your love and a sense of their own selves through the finger-work. Touching, tasting, smelling, seeing, hearing are primary activities for the before-school child. This is his natural environment for learning. Let him taste the cake batter, smell autumn leaves and wood burning, hear traffic sounds, see the stars and the dog's nose, touch velvet and sandpaper by sharing those experiences with him and being aware of them yourself.

Try to take five minutes a day with each child for his own sharing with you. Your pre-school may be

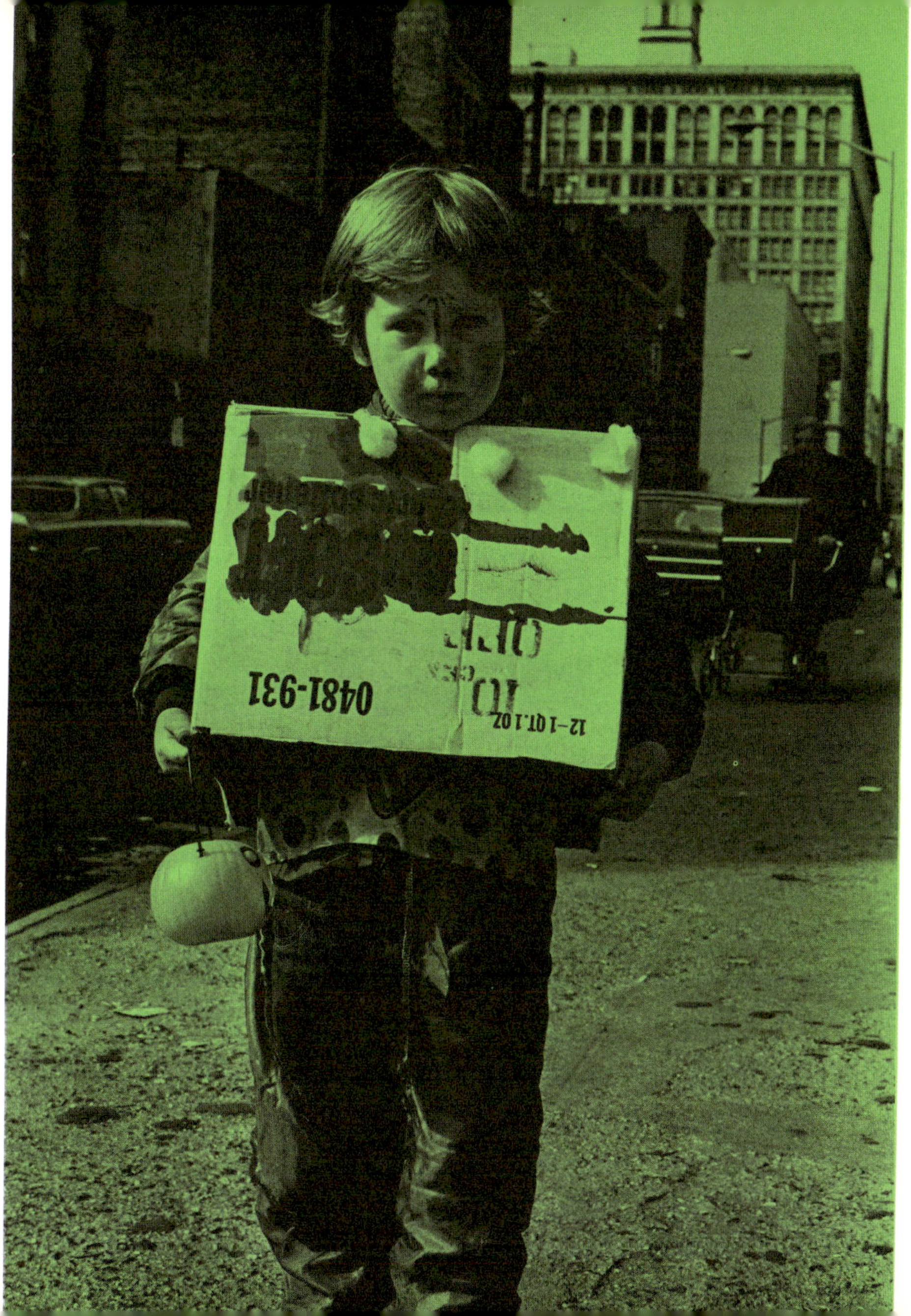
0481-931
12-1 QT.1 OZ

the one neglected because he is with you so much. Stop the housework, television, sewing, whatever—and just sit down with him for some sharing.

New books for parents who want to work with their children are Dolores Curran's *Who, Me? Teach My Child Religion* (Minex Publications); Charles M. Schulz (yes, he is the Peanuts man) has written a wonderful book called *Two-by-fours* (age two-four) which has some basic rules for children of that age and religion (Warner Press, Anderson, Indiana). Anything from Sesame Street makes children perk up. A catalog from the Preschool Press has articles for sale plus some good theory and ideas.

By instilling in our children a sense of wonder and reverence, we are preparing them to become concerned about the whole world for which they as adults will be responsible. Each day is another formative one in shaping the kind of persons our children will become. Each day each of us can begin anew; each day each of us is changed from what we were the day before, and tomorrow something new will be a part of our lives. For the children of tomorrow, this truth is dramatically so—much more so than when today's adults were growing up.

If we want them to grow into loving, responsible, sensitive persons—into mature Christians—we want to help them form a vision of life that will foster in them the strengths and hopes with which they can meet the future which lies so mysterious, so uncharted for our future generations.

To do this, we want to encourage in our children enthusiasm, the sparkle of delight in discovering new worlds every day, a curiosity to ponder what it's all about and to never rest satisfied with half-answers, an abiding faith and hope in the goodness of God and of men, and the belief that there is an ultimate reason for all of this that is both pain and joy. And, hopefully, we will foster in them a creative responsibility for altering and shaping the world and its structures.

It is only a mature person, one with vision enough to see beyond the human problems without discouragement or despair, who will attempt to build a better world, who will attempt to give to that world and others his own gifts of beauty and strength and talent, gifts which are uniquely and preciously his own and which no other person can give. Such is the dream we have for our children.

U.S.A